Praise for Adam Bolivar and *Ballads for the Witching Hour*

Ballads for the Witching Hour is a glorious exploration of a rediscovered form; a form that can never quite die. Truly poetic balladry will always shimmer through from the misty realm of living shadows. Adam Bolivar is the modern Burns of this form. He has mastered balladry and he enraptures us with eerily glowing tales wrought seamlessly within it.—John Shirley, author of *The Voice of the Burning House.*

"To read the work of Adam Bolivar is to enter an enchanted realm of pure poetry, where skill is combined with a brilliant imagination. Superb!"—W. H. Pugmire, author of *Uncommon Places.*

"Adam Bolivar offers a unique blend of folktale, fantasy and pure cosmic horror.... High entertainment for any fan of the fantastic!"—Ann K. Schwader, author of *Dark Energies.*

"The spectral balladry of Adam Bolivar is a refreshing adaptation of the ballads of Sir Walter Scott, Thomas Moore, and other Romantic poets who found in them an ideal vehicle for the powerful expression of weird moods and imagery. Bolivar's flawless metre and smooth-flowing stanzas create a sense of cumulative terror and strangeness easily rivaling the best work of contemporary weird fiction writers."—S. T. Joshi.

Ballads for the Witching Hour

Tam O'Shanter by William Brassey Hole,
from *The Poetry of Robert Burns,* vol. I, Edinburgh, 1897.

Ballads for the Witching Hour

❁

Rimes, Lays, and
Plays for Marionettes

Adam Bolivar

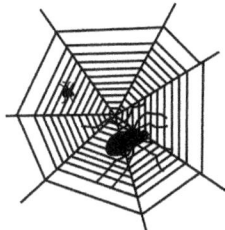

Hippocampus Press

New York

Published by Hippocampus Press
P.O. Box 641, New York, NY 10156.
www.hippocampuspress.com

Cover by Daniel V. Sauer, dansauerdesign.com, incorporating
Tam O'Shanter and the Witches by John Faed (1892).
Hippocampus Press logo designed by Anastasia Damianakos.

First Edition
1 3 5 7 9 8 6 4 2

ISBN: 978-1-61498-388-0 paperback
ISBN: 978-1-61498-394-1 ebook

Contents

On Balladry

Foremost among poetic forms, the ballad evokes the haunted relics of folklore: witches, faeries, hellhounds, the jealous sister, the murdered lover, and tales of Jack and the Devil. Close kin to fairy tales, such ballads as "Tam-Lin" and "Thomas the Rhymer" would be right at home in the collections of the Brothers Grimm or Charles Perrault's *Contes de ma mère l'Oye.*

In fourteenth- and fifteenth-century Britain, ballads were a ubiquitous form of entertainment, crooned by harp-strumming minstrels to nobles in their halls, and belted out by peasants in taverns. The idle priest in *Piers Plowman* may not have remembered his paternoster, but well he knew the "rymes of Robyn Hood." With the advent of the printing press at the end of the fifteenth century, ballads were distributed as cheaply printed broadsides to be sung at home to well-worn tunes. Old traditional ballads were printed alongside newly (and often poorly) composed ones, or patchwork pastiches of the two, contributing to a decline in quality. By the age of Shakespeare, ballads had fallen out of fashion among those of more refined taste, though they were perennially popular with the masses. It was only with the publication of such scholarly works as Thomas Percy's *Reliques of Ancient English Poetry* (1765), Robert Harley's *Roxburgh Ballads* (1784), and Sir Walter Scott's *Minstrelsy of the Scottish Border* (1802) that the reputation of the ballad was restored.

Beginning with the 1798 publication of *Lyrical Ballads* by Samuel Taylor Coleridge and William Wordsworth, they and other nineteenth-century poets such as John Keats, Christina Rossetti, Elizabeth Barrett Browning, Alfred, Lord Tennyson, and Algernon Charles Swinburne found inspiration in the ballad and adopted the metrical form in their own works: *The Rime of the Ancient Mariner,* "Lines Written a Few Miles Above Tintern Abbey," "La Belle Dame Sans Merci," *Goblin Market,* "The Lady of Shalott," and "The Garden of Proserpine" to name a few.

The great ballad scholar Francis James Child, whose still-definitive five-volume collection, *The English and Scottish Popular Ballads,* was published between 1882 and 1898, was bedeviled by the corruption of true "folk" poetry by later inventions and reinventions, and he did his best to separate the two. However, in his book *The Ballad Revival* (1961), Albert B. Friedman argues that such a distinction is not so clear. Folk traditions are influenced by written material and vice versa. Consider the case of "The Knoxville Girl." A ballad was composed about the brutal murder of Anne Nichols near Shrewsbury in 1683 and distributed as a broadside. When the broadside was reprinted abroad, the setting of the murder was shifted to appeal to local readers. In Ireland, the ballad became "The Wexford Girl"; in Tennessee, "The Knoxville Girl." These far-flung variants passed into collective memory as folk songs, which were later set to print once more, transmuted by the alchemy of time, yet uncannily faithful to the original truth.

So perhaps the old woman erred when she told Sir Walter Scott that if he printed her ballads they would be "never be sung mair." The magic in the ballad is hardier than that. It can lie in wait in the printed word, for centuries if need be, until it is planted anew in the fertile soil of a receptive mind. The silver gates to Faerie will never entirely be closed to us so long as ballads are read and sung.

Jack's Alive. A number of people sit in a row, or in chairs round a parlour. A lighted wooden spill or taper is handed to the first, who says—

> *Jack's alive, and likely to live;*
> *If he dies in your hand you've a forfeit to give.*

The one in whose hand the light expires has to pay a forfeit. As the spill is getting burnt out the lines are said very quickly, as everybody is anxious not to have to pay the forfeit.

—Addy's *Sheffield Glossary,* 1888

* * *

"Jack ain't dead. He's a-livin'. Jack can be anybody. Like I tell 'em sometimes, I'm Jack. Now I ain't done everything Jack has done in the tales, but still I've been Jack in a lot of ways. It takes Jack to live."

—Ray Hicks, traditional teller of Jack tales,
Beech Mountain, North Carolina, 1983

* * *

"This little dog does nothing, but I hope he will mend; he is now reading Jack the Giant-killer. Perhaps so noble a narrative may rouse in him the soul of enterprise."

—Samuel Johnson to Mrs. Thrale, March 14, 1768

* * *

Jack be nimble,
Jack be quick,
Jack jump over
The candlestick.
—English nursery rhyme

To Her Ineffable Majeſtie,

Y^E QUEENE OF ELPHAME

I.
Ballads for the Witching Hour

Sing ballads for the witching hour,
    O Scarlet Balladress,
Thou dewy crimson petalled flow'r,
    Beguiling sorceress,

Out here amongst the goblin stones,
    All standing in a ring,
Where gather crooked crooning crones
    The Otherworld to bring.

Sing ballads for the witching hour,
    O Balladress, my queen,
While in the shadows I shall cow'r
    For fear of being seen.

Now pixies come to dance in threes,
    'Neath stars that whirl above,
A sight that brings me to me knees,
    Tears falling and in love.

A dream-gate opens mid the stones:
    The Balladress steps through;
Her ballads ended, chill in bones,
    I bid the stones adieu.

II.
The King of Cats

As I was walking in the wood
    I came upon a place
Where once a manor house had stood,
    And now a thorn-grown space

In which a funeral of cats
    With reverence laid to rest
A coffin carven with a crown,
    Its workmanship the best.

Well, I was horror-stricken by
    This supernatural scene,
And hastened from that haunted spot,
    Half-mad from what I'd seen.

But this affair compelled me then
    To call upon a friend
And tell him of the strangeness that
    Few poets could have penned.

Well, scarcely had my tale been told
    When I a marvel saw:
A cat that slept before the fire
    Quite archly raised a paw:

II. THE KING OF CATS

'Then I am King of Cats,' he said,
And with a blinding flash
A-scrambled up the chimney flue,
While I choked on the ash.

III.
The Hounds

A village huddled by a moor
    Was haunted by the sounds,
Which all who lived there did deplore:
    The baying of the hounds.

Some years ago there lived a squire,
    A wicked man and tight,
Whose reputation in the shire
    Was black as barley blight.

Jack's hall was cold as was his heart,
    Of friends he counted none;
Some say he practiced devil's art
    And loathed to see the sun.

His fiendish ways came at a price,
    Incarnate in the hounds,
Whose howls would freeze his blood to ice,
    Abhorrent were the sounds.

For as Jack's coffers waxed with gold,
    And Mollys warmed his bed,
His skin and bones grew very cold
    Like one nigh unto dead—

III. THE HOUNDS

A hound for ev'ry unborn child
  This loathsome rake would sire
On maidens whom he had defiled
  With his depraved desire.

At last the Devil came for Jack
  To feed him to the hounds,
Which ran behind his hearse of black
  And made infernal sounds.

They chase behind this carriage still,
  Which Jack is said to drive
Across the moor in deathless chill,
  His slumber to deprive.

IV.
The Duke of Balladry

On Balladry, the Sapphire Isle,
    A castle, ruined, stands,
A haunted brooding ancient pile
    Upon bejewelled sands.

He is the Duke of Balladry,
    The master of this isle,
Whose name resounds in legendry
    And regal is his style;

For secretly, as ravens know,
    He is the King of Nod,
His ballads known to any crow,
    And widely are they cawed.

While underneath and in the end
    His secret name is Jack:
To dreamers all he is a friend
    Who tread the Ancient Track.

V.
The Ballad Stone

The Ballad Stone is moody blue,
    A goblin-chiselled gem,
A sapphire of uncanny hue
    Upon a diadem

That once adorned a pixie queen
    And now a ducal crown,
Which though it seldom now is seen
    Has garnered great renown.

Who wears it hears a spectre sing
    Strange ballads very old,
While pixies gambol in a ring—
    Or so the tale is told.

This phantom strums on silver strings
    That drive their hearer mad,
Who sees then insubstantial things
    And dancers all unclad.

These pixies dance and sing of Jack,
    Their lover sweet and fair,
Who wanders down the Ancient Track
    With wild and flowing hair.

V. THE BALLAD STONE

The Ballad Duke soon joined their dance,
 For Jack he also was,
Who only cared to find Romance,
 Disdainful of God's laws.

VI.
The Crimson Harp

There dwelt upon a sapphire isle
    A languid dreamy duke
Who all his nighttime hours would wile
    Away without rebuke.

He had a lyre from ancient times
    That sang of ballads lost;
To hearken to its haunted rimes
    Came at exquisite cost.

Stained crimson was this vampire harp
    With blood once scarlet red
Spilled by a knife that was so sharp
    It cut its owner dead.

And when of blood it had a taste,
    The lyre craved ever more
From ladies who had been disgraced
    And men caught with a whore.

Two sisters walked beside the sea:
    One pushed the other in;
It was the rage of jealousy
    That drove her to this sin.

VI. THE CRIMSON HARP

A bloody chamber had a squire
  With women's bones a-filled;
Alas, their tale was very dire,
  The wives that he had killed.

Mad Jack-a-Lee with swagger came,
  And to a tavern strode
To crow to all his hateful name
  Before the blood a-flowed.

These ballads did the duke long hear,
  Of murders cruel and red;
Like brands into his heart would sear
  These sorrows of the dead.

At last the cock a-crowed the morn
  To send the duke to bed,
Though evermore he was forlorn
  His dreams he e'er would dread.

VII.
The Haunting Bones

Two sisters by a river strolled,
    The winding River Tay,
Beneath which dwells a beast of old,
    Or so the legends say.

The dark one pushed the fair one in:
    It was a jealous rage
That led her to commit this sin
    And nothing could assuage;

For handsome Jack the fair one loved,
    And she would marry him,
And so the dark one swiftly shoved
    Her sister on a whim.

The poor girl sank into the murk,
    Which gratified the beast
Who underneath was said to lurk
    And hunger for a feast.

When came the spring a minstrel found
    Upon the bank her bones
To craft a harp that had a sound
    Quite haunting in its tones.

VIII. The Haunting Bones

Invited to a wedding feast
    The balladeer then was,
An irony that pleased the Beast
    Who was this mischief's cause.

The sister who had hair of black,
    And was a murderess,
Was marrying now handsome Jack
    And wore a silken dress.

The balladeer the bone-harp played,
    Æthereal the sound;
A ghost in tatters all arrayed
    Bewailed: the girl who drowned—

'I once was Elspeth, fair of tress,
    Betrothed this day to wed;
I ought to wear that silken dress—
    Alas, but I am dead.

'My sister Eleanora killed
    Me out of lust for Jack;
My heart beneath the Tay was stilled,
    For hers was cold and black.'

VII. THE HAUNTING BONES

Then Eleanora fled the hall,
    And nevermore was heard;
And ever would that harp enthrall
    When were the bones bestirred.

VIII.
Mad Jack-a-Lee

Mad Jack-a-Lee to Hexham came
    With blood upon his boots;
The laws of men could never tame
    The wildness in his roots.

At crossing roads he found an inn
    And thought to take a drink;
From travelling he was bone-thin—
    A skeleton you'd think.

Inside the inn was thick with smoke,
    A noxious swirling haze;
Jack strode across the creaking oak
    And caught the barman's gaze.

'A pint of ale or maybe two,'
    He said as cold as ice.
'My name is Jack, I say to you;
    Don't make me say it twice.'

A Balladress upon the stage
    Strummed on a black guitar,
Emballading Jack's scarlet rage
    As she watched from afar.

VIII. Mad Jack-a-Lee

'And for this ale how will you pay?'
    The barman asked of Jack,
And no more words would e'er he say,
    For came a pistol's crack.

The barman's blood ran dark and red,
    Like wine that had been spilled,
And now he lay, his spirit fled,
    The latest Jack had killed.

Jack lay his gun upon the bar
    And helped himself to rye;
He thought of those he'd killed in war,
    The men he'd left to die.

The Balladress was hot as flame
    And burned for love of Jack,
Though never would he feel the same—
    His heart was cold and black.

A devil came to steal Jack's soul,
    A woman crimson dressed;
Her eyes were cruel and black as coal,
    And lily was her breast.

VIII. MAD JACK-A-LEE

Jack stopped and turned a merry dance—
    You should have heard them moan;
It made the singer turn askance
    And feel then all alone.

And when this wicked deed was done,
    No silver coin was paid;
Jack took in hand his iron gun
    And shot the crimson maid.

The Balladress resumed her tune
    And caught Jack by the eye;
He left her there lit by the moon,
    The one who didn't die.

IX.
The Jack of Cats

The King of Cats prowled through the wood
    Towards a haunting tune,
Till Fiddler Jack before him stood
    And played beneath the moon.

He played and played and played some more,
    While pixies danced in threes;
He played so well the Cat King swore
    To knight him on his knees.

So Jack knelt down before the King,
    Who dubbed him with a paw,
And then he raised his voice to sing,
    While silence fell in awe.

'I am a knight, a Jack of Cats,
    So noble now my name
That all will bow and doff their hats
    And murmur of my fame.'

X.
The Scarlet Room

There was a squire whose name was Fox,
    Whose house was grand and old;
He kept a room of bloody frocks
    In which lay bones grown cold.

He wooed a lady, Mary Drake,
    That charming gallant squire,
A handsome figure did he make,
    A profile to admire.

A wedding day was set, of course:
    The coming Eve of May,
Upon the moor amongst the gorse
    To make the bride's bouquet.

Squire Fox's house lay in the wood,
    Though Mary saw it not;
She knew as long as it had stood,
    Dark legends it had brought.

When her betrothed had gone away,
    She ventured to the wood
To learn if what she had heard say
    Had been misunderstood.

X. THE SCARLET ROOM

The House of Fox at length she found,
    A castle, very old,
Which ancient forest did surround
    And legendry was told.

Above the gate with writ the words:
    'Be bold, my dear, be bold.'
And in the hall were many swords;
    Stark fear on her took hold.

She found a door atop the stair
    And tried then to be bold;
For what she saw inside of there
    Would make her blood run cold.

A secret chamber lay within
    With scarlet bones all filled,
A place the squire hid blackest sin,
    The wives that he had killed.

Then Mary heard a piercing shriek
    And hid behind a cask;
She raised her head to take a peek,
    Her face a startled mask.

X. The Scarlet Room

Squire Fox, her love, betrothed to her,
    Dragged in another maid
Who flailed and cried and made a stir,
    For she was so afraid.

The blackguard cut her hand from her
    To get a ruby ring.
In Mary's lap it landed, sir,
    A most uncanny thing!

Then Mary fled that wicked room,
    Her lap now crimson stained;
Come morn Squire Fox would be her groom,
    By wedding bonds enchained.

Well, at the breakfast feast she said
    That she had had a dream,
That she had found a room so red,
    The blood flowed in a stream.

'Alas, it is not so, my dear,'
    Said Squire Fox, her groom.
'It was a dream, so have no fear
    Of any scarlet room.'

X. THE SCARLET ROOM

'Into that room you dragged your wife,
    Upon her hand a ring;
To get it you would take her life
    And gave your sword a swing.'

'A dream, a dream, that's all it was,'
    Squire Fox to her demurred.
'And of such tales there is no cause;
    I say they are absurd!'

'But here's the ring, that ruby ring,
    Upon the lady's hand;
Your line I vow a taint will bring
    Upon our pleasant land.'

Then Lady Mary's kindred all
    The wicked Fox cut down;
That Eve of May his line would fall,
    And crimson Mary's gown.

XI.
The Ballad God

There is a meadow, Fiddler's Green,
    Deep in the Land of Nod,
Where pixies go to dance unseen
    Before the Ballad God,

Who plays a ghoulish harp of bones;
    Disquieting, this lyre,
Its silver strings invoking tones
    That madness can inspire.

He makes the pixies sway and gyre
    Before an orange fire,
While Luna rises higher—higher!—
    And frogs croak in the mire.

All hail the Ballad God! Hail Pan,
    Who woman twines with man
In faunish ways that lovers can
    And have since time began.

Who seeks for him is such a fool—
    Alas, this fool am I!
His inspiration savage, cruel,
    Who follows him must die.

XI. The Ballad God

But never is such rapture found
 As in that moonlit mead,
Which echoes with a lyre's sound,
 While frogs croak in the reed.

XII.
The Queen of Cats

There was a Scarlet Balladress
    Who strummed a black guitar;
In cloak arrayed, and wild of tress,
    Her ballads carried far.

One night she stopped in Cuckoo's Wood
    To sleep beside a stream;
She shivered, drawing up her hood,
    Half waking, half in dream.

A cat appeared and doffed his hat,
    A fiddle in his paw;
He played a haunted lyric that
    Affronted natural law.

The Balladress then took her turn
    And played her song of Jack,
For whom her heart will ever yearn,
    A harking void and black.

'O Jack, my love, my only one,
    I sing this song for you;
Long roads I've walked, strange games I've won
    To prove my love is true.

XII. THE QUEEN OF CATS

'The Devil promised by his horn
　　To guide me to my love,
And hearth and home I have forsworn,
　　My roof the stars above.'

Her victory the cat confessed
　　And knelt before his Queen,
This Balladress in scarlet dressed,
　　This tangle-haired colleen.

XIII.
The House That Jack Built

A Play for Marionettes

*** Dramatis Personae ***

JACK STRAW, a scarecrow
SOLOMON SCRATCH, a travelling salesman of sorts
The Time: The days of yore
The Place: A gone but not forgotten cornfield

*
*
* * *
*

A Diabolical Tragedy in Four Acts

ACT ONE

JACK Straw is hanging from a post in a cornfield. A house looms in the background.

JACK: O happy day which over me dawns;
                The white cock crows and the black crow caws.
                A simple Jack Straw I sit on my post,
                A-scarin' the crows for this I love most.

SCRATCH: Good morning, good sir, what glorious weather!
                I feel I could dance, as light as a feather.
                Allow me to introduce myself: Solomon Scratch is my name;
                And the striking of deals my unspeakable game.

	Do you want wine, women and power,
	Stacks of gold piled high in a tower?
	Just sign your name in Olde Solomon's Booke,
	And who can deny 'tis I who's been took?

JACK: Well, Mr. Scratch, you're barkin' up the wrong tree,
For I love scarin' crows and the farmers, they love me.

SCRATCH: Scaring crows? Humbug, my friend.
This field is abandoned, kaput, a dead-end.
The farmers are gone, packed up and skipped town;
They left you to swing, for none took you down.

JACK: The farmers are gone? Left town did you say?
I'd wondered why no one was planting in May . . .

SCRATCH: You need a new outfit, some spring in your step.
It's time you got cracking. How long have you slept?

JACK: Upon my whole life you've shed a new light;
Good golly miss molly, why maybe you're right.

SCRATCH: Wouldn't it please you to dance and to play?
To gambol amidst the lilies of May?
And not be affixed to a pole in a field?
I can give you these things . . . only your soul you must yield.

JACK: To fill my jug with songs in a tavern?
Finding a treasure trove of gold in a cavern . . .

SCRATCH: (aside) My oath, my spurs & garters, my burning ears,
Could these be the words of a deal that I hear?

JACK: To have these things I'd sign in a second—
To have these things a deal could be reckoned . . .

SCRATCH: To business then—
I know of a spell, a black spell, a spell
Treasured by the Ancient Ones,
Hoarded by the More Ancient Ones,
for it had been so cunningly and
ingeniously contrived by the
Still More Ancient Ones
Before Them . . .

It is spell which can turn straw to a man,
I'll say it aloud to see if I can:

Eenie meenie miney moe,
Catch a scarecrow by the toe;
If he hollers let him go,
Out goes WHY-OH-
YAN-TAN-Teth-
Era. Quid-
Pro-quo
Cada
Bra;
AMEN.
Shang-die, Shang-do;
Out goes Y-O-U!

JACK is freed from his post.

SCRATCH: Arise from your roost, gentle Jack o' the Straw;
Your pastures are nigh, my word is the law.

JACK takes his first steps.

SCRATCH: Not straw, now a man, my handsomest prince,
The fairest I've seen of many I've since.

	Take you this pipe of Black Mary's Weed
	For it shall give you the strength that you need.

JACK: Oh, thank you, Mr. Scratch. God bless you. Amen.
A happy man I am as happy as a clam,
To dance around in grass
And frolic like a lamb.
O what more could I possibly ask
Than to play around in sunlight and bask?

SCRATCH: It tickles me pink, a job so well done.
But we'll see how you fare for a year in the sun.
Come back in one year, come back to this spot,
And tell Master Scratch how you've fared with your lot.
I'll wait for you here, as heavy as lead,
Right here on this spot scaring crows in your stead.

Exit JACK.

ACT TWO

SCRATCH is waiting by the post. Enter JACK.

SCRATCH: At last good Jack, I say you are late.
You do know how much I so hate to wait.

JACK: O Master Scratch, I have been so far and so wide . . .
There's a spring in my step, a strength in my stride.

SCRATCH: That much is apparent. Tell on.

JACK: I have been to the palace of King Prester John,
And melted his heart with my dance and my song.
I have seen the brooding face of the Sphinx,
And the Land of Nod where lotus-blooms wink.

SCRATCH: You don't say? (yawns)

JACK: I have knelt before the feet of a queen . . .
           My heart races madly for all I have seen!

SCRATCH: Hmm. How touching.
           And what have you learned in all this skedaddle?
           Have you a clue? Or is it all prattle?

JACK: A clue? Why, what do you mean, Master Scratch?

SCRATCH: A clue, dear boy, some horse sense, some savvy.
           Answer me quickly, and don't dilly-dally—
           What is the one thing the whole world goes round?
           I'll give you a hint . . . a jingling sound.

JACK: Umm . . . gravity?

SCRATCH: Uh-uh. No dice. I'm sorry. You lose.
           There must be somebody else I can use . . .

SCRATCH turns to leave.

JACK: No, wait . . . don't go . . .
           This sounds important. I want to know.

SCRATCH: Want? Need, dear boy. This one simple fact.
           Money's the key to all your doors, Jack.

JACK: Money?

SCRATCH: Moolah. Simoleons. Greenbacks. Dinero.
           My, you'd look good in a brand new sombrero.

JACK: Gee, this one is gettin' old . . .

SCRATCH: I can array you in the finest of robes,
           And rid you of these rags you must loathe!
           In your tower I can stack a fortune in gold,
           And silver and jewels and riches untold!

JACK:	All that for li'l ol' me?
SCRATCH:	You have but to ask me whose soul you have lent. I do it for love and charge not a cent.
JACK:	You make me an offer I cannot refuse . . . Sure, I'll take your gold. Heck, I've got nothing to lose.
SCRATCH:	Take you this bag of Red Vulcan's Gold. It can never be emptied, or so I've been told. Arise from your riches, Sir Jack o' the Straw. Your riches are nigh, my word is the law.
JACK:	My lord, my gratitude is without measure; How happy I am to take of my leisure.
SCRATCH:	It tickles me pink a job so well done, But we'll see how you fare with your cup overrun. Come back in one year. Come back to this spot. And tell Master Scratch how you've fared with your lot.

Exit JACK.

ACT THREE

SCRATCH is still waiting. Enter JACK.

SCRATCH:	My dear Jack, you are dressed to the nines, With an air of dignity and manners refined. Has the luxury of the rich and entitled Suited you to a life so carefree and idle?
JACK:	Master Scratch, at the richest of tables have I dined, Eating rare feasts and sampling wines. I have won whole kingdoms in cards, To find the next night them lying in shards.

SCRATCH: (aside) His gut is a hole which never gets filled;
If he goes on this way methinks he'll be killed . . .

JACK: I have tasted of the pleasures of whores,
Tempted by ladies who stand under doors.
I have drunk the potions which make men see stars,
And scried my own future in Saturn and Mars.
Yet the more I have the more I crave;
Grant me this boon and I'll be your slave.

SCRATCH: Will be? (chuckles)
Well, Old Uncle Scratch has a big bag of tricks.
Perhaps in his bag my toy can be fixed.

JACK: O would I were lord of my very own manor,
And waving above my proudly sewn banner.
Can you give me the key to this house,
And servants to toy with as a cat does a mouse?

SCRATCH: A tall order you make, but let me see—
Perhaps in my bag I have an old key . . .
Kneel.

JACK kneels.
Cue: Lower key.

SCRATCH: Ahem. By the power vested in me
By the Principate of Pandaemonium,
I hereby name you:
Marquis of Oxford, Baron
of Wittenberg, Elector
of Worms, and Count of Cordova . . .
Arise as a peer, Lord Jack o' the Straw;
Your key to the house, my word is the law.

JACK: Master Scratch, how can I ever you repay?
               I'd give you my soul . . .

SCRATCH: Would? Heh-heh.

JACK: I'd give you anything . . . whatever you say.

SCRATCH: My dear child, my work is its own reward.
               But perhaps there is one honor you could me award.

JACK: You have but to name it, sire.

SCRATCH: Should ever again I pass by this way,
               Be it October, or be it in May,
               Will you take me to warm at your hearth
               As one who is dearest to your noble heart?

JACK: My oath, Master Scratch, t'would be a great pleasure
               To honor the one who's bestow'd me such treasure.

SCRATCH: Tempus fugit and me I must fly.
               Perhaps in ten years I'll come and drop by . . .

Exit SCRATCH.

ACT FOUR

Enter SCRATCH. There is a knock on the door.

Enter JACK.

JACK: Who awakes me at this time of night,
               Disturbing my peace with such a loud fright?

SCRATCH: 'Tis I, Old Solomon Scratch come to call.
               I've come to sit and dine at your hall.

JACK: Solomon Scratch? The name rings a bell . . .
               Aren't you the devil of whom I've heard tell?

SCRATCH:	Devil or not, you struck me a deal.
	I gave you this house, now give me a meal!
JACK:	A deal with the devil? Oh, what was I thinking?
	I must have been mad—or up all night drinking.
SCRATCH:	Your tune has changed, Lord Jack o' the Straw.
	I knew that it would. Your word has no law.
JACK:	Begone from my house, you filthy old demon!
	For I have a name to uphold with the freemen . . .
SCRATCH:	Ungrateful wretch, without me you'd have no name,
	For Jack Straw and Scarecrow are one and the same.
JACK:	Fie! You bat, you snake, you two-tongued devil!
	Get thee hence, back to the fires of hell!
SCRATCH:	Enough! From all that I've heard,
	I know you a Tom Fool who can't keep his word.
	Never a man but always of straw
	My spell was a sham. I laugh. I guffaw.
JACK:	A sham? But what of the pipe of Black Mary's Weed?
SCRATCH:	Black Mary's Weed? That's a laugh—
	Where I come from son, they call the stuff grass.
JACK:	And the gold . . .
SCRATCH:	The never-ending gold which comes from a bag?
	I stuffed a few pebbles inside a torn rag.
JACK:	Get out of my house before I call the local constabulary!

SCRATCH: Your house?
             Your house is a shambles,
             All grown over by brambles—
             Your house is a-falling, so sit very tight;
             Your house is a-falling; I bid you good night . . .

JACK is bound to the post again.

SCRATCH: What comes from straw to straw must return,
             And you shall know what it means to BURN!

Lower HELLMOUTH backdrop.

JACK: Mercy!

SCRATCH: The deal is struck; the straw is burned;
             The gate is closed; the key is turned.

SCRATCH bows.

Lower curtain.

*** THE END ***

XIV.
Cat's Paw

Jack wandered down the Ancient Track,
 Which passed a ruined mill;
The woods around were thick and black
 And brought his bones a chill.

He sheltered there, all travel-sore,
 And cooked himself some meat;
A black cat slunk across the floor
 Upon four padded feet.

Twelve more black cats from windows glared,
 Their eyes a-glowing green,
Their backs were arched, their fangs were bared,
 Their caterwauls obscene.

The cat outstretched her paw toward
 The pan to snag Jack's beef;
A silver knife's edge her reward:
 The wages of a thief.

The cat cried 'wa-r-r-r-r-r!' and quit her plan—
 The others followed suit;
A witch's hand lay in the pan,
 And gave Jack a salute.

XV.
Jack and the Devil

Hear now the tale of Jack the Smith,
　　　　To Wayland nigh a match;
And though some say it was a myth,
　　　　He once outwit Old Scratch.

Some say Jack was a wicked man
　　　　Who never went to church;
His life so grim he made a plan
　　　　To dangle from a birch.

But in the wood the Devil came
　　　　To offer Jack a deal:
If in a book he'd write his name
　　　　And spill his blood to seal,

The Devil would do Jack a turn
　　　　Bestowing riches vast,
And afterwards Jack's soul would burn
　　　　When twenty years had passed.

Well, Jack went home and found a chest,
　　　　Brim-filled with jewels and gold,
Which matched his station with the best
　　　　Of any in the Wold.

XV. Jack and the Devil

So wickedly Jack led his life
    His name was wed with sin,
And ev'ry night another wife
    Was taken at the inn.

A grey old man one afternoon
    A-wandered by Jack's forge;
Jack kindly offered him the boon
    Of letting him engorge

On fresh baked bread and wine and meat,
    For generous Jack was,
And any who had need to eat
    Jack let him fill his jaws.

In truth a god this rambler was
    And gave to Jack a chair,
Which bound and rocked without a pause
    Whoever might sit there.

Now when the devil came to call
    To take the debt come due,
Jack asked a moment that he stall
    To forge a half-formed shoe.

XV. JACK AND THE DEVIL

So while he waited for the smith,
    Scratch sat upon the chair,
Which bound the demon there forthwith,
    A madly rocking snare.

At last the Devil mercy pled
    And Jack laid out his terms:
To tear the page on which he'd bled
    From out the Book of Worms.

Old Scratch agreed to do this deed
    And from the chair he sprang—
To run away with such great speed,
    The children jeered and sang.

XVI.
The Black Hunt

On Hallowe'en a hunter rides
      With hounds as black as coal;
And like a fox who slinks and hides,
      His quarry is a soul

That flickers like a lanthorn's light
      Deep in the Yellow'd Reed;
You'll see it in the moonless night,
      And mimicked in a swede.

'Tis Jack for whom the dark man hunts,
      This rider all in black,
For there is none who so affronts
      The Devil as spry Jack.

For once Jack kissed the Devil's wife,
      Pale Lilith's crimson lips,
And then I swear upon my life,
      He slipped between her hips—

So now Jack flees the rider's wrath
      And hides deep in the reed,
For like a hare he knows the path
      To shun the hounds with speed.

XVI. THE BLACK HUNT

And there he waits until the light
When dawns All Hallow's Day;
The hunter then will take his flight,
The hounds will fade away.

XVII.
The House of Gloom

I tell of Jack, who blew the horn
    To wake the giant in the morn,
Whose clothes are old and tattertorn,
    Who seeks the Tower in the thorn.

He left the inn, the Toad and Crow,
    His countenance forlorn,
For he had nothing left to blow
    Now that he'd lost his horn.

Jack journeyed onward down the road
    In hopes his fortune turned;
A vision to him was bestowed,
    Since childhood had it burned:

Within a Tower's garret wait
    A Lady with a Cup;
But first Jack had to pass the gate
    Before he could climb up.

He heard an owl hoot in the day—
    An omen, to be sure;
Jack felt that he had lost his way,
    His heart become impure.

XVII. THE HOUSE OF GLOOM

The thorn-hemmed path wound on and on;
    Jack slowly down it crept;
The hell-mouth opened in a yawn
    While angels softly wept.

He found himself in yellow'd reed,
    A marshy, mazy place,
A place a rampant hare would lead
    If any give him chase.

Beyond the reed there lay a pond
    Where willows swayed and bent,
Where frogs in legions came to spawn,
    Where lilies wafted scent.

Beside the pond, a rain-worn stone
    In which was carved the name
Of Mary who once sat alone,
    And dreamt she played a game.

Beyond the pond a marble tomb,
    A hoary crumbling vault;
Who lay inside had met their doom—
    This insight made Jack halt.

XVII. The House of Gloom

Quietus came for all one day
    But would not come for him,
For Jack was favoured by the fey,
    Enduring at their whim.

I do not mean this mortal coil,
    For Jack like all must die;
But underneath the fertile soil
    He never long would lie.

His spirit was a blazing fire,
    Called Iakkios of old;
By nature he would never tire
    Of hearing Jack-tales told.

Jack cheated death and was reborn,
    An infant, squalling, new;
And when he came of age a horn
    His purpose would imbue.

Then from the tomb Jack turned away;
    The charnel stench was vile;
The noxious odour of decay
    Did little to beguile.

XVII. The House of Gloom

Before him loomed Old Ettinfell,
    The fallen house of Drake,
Whose souls abode in darkest hell
    Till Golden Dawn a-break.

Jack strode up to the rotting door
    Of once-stout oaken beams;
The ancient arms of Drake loomed o'er,
    A wyrm from fitful dreams.

Well, who should open up that door
    But long-eared Harold Gloom?
Jack stepped upon the creaking floor,
    Which echoed like a tomb.

'The House of Drake is now of Gloom,'
    Then Harold smugly said.
'The last Drake willed it with a plume
    Before collapsing dead.'

His tenure Jack did not protest,
    Or call the hare a cheat;
He only asked a place to rest
    And for a bite to eat.

XVII. The House of Gloom

Begrudgingly Gloom played the host
    And fed Jack in the hall
A crust of bread without a roast,
    And even that was small.

And then he took Jack to a room,
    Its furnishings austere;
Such was the welcome of the Gloom,
    A courtesy most queer.

But when the hour of witches chimed,
    Jack crept out of his room,
And up the stairs he softly climbed,
    Neglected by the broom.

Jack opened up the attic door
    By turning thrice the key;
He'd learned this secret scrap of lore
    Upon his beldam's knee.

He felt he had been here before,
    Inside this attic room,
And so he entered it once more,
    Atop the House of Gloom.

XVII. The House of Gloom

Upon the writing desk a book,
　　Embossed a cruel design:
A horned black shepherd with a crook—
　　It was the Crimson Sign.

Well, Jack the game would not give up;
　　He played his final card:
The Lady waiting with the Cup,
　　Whose path and Jack's were starred.

The seven-angled sign he drew
　　Upon a virgin page;
The magick from his fingers flew,
　　A skilled and potent mage.

For Jack had something Harold lacked:
　　The ancient blood of Drake;
He spilt a drop and by that act,
　　Winged Dumah stirred awake.

The Angel carried Jack aloft
　　Into a barren land,
And like a feather landed soft
　　Upon the shifting sand.

XVII. THE HOUSE OF GLOOM

The Tower loomed, so dark and old,
    Jack stormed up to the gate;
His blood was stirring, hot and bold,
    Athirst to meet his fate.

The Silver Key he jammed and turned
    Inside the iron lock;
His efforts, though, the tumblers spurned—
    The gate, a fractious block.

And then it dawned. Alas! Alack!
    He had no horn to blow.
The Tower faded into black
    While starkly laughed a crow.

Once more in Darkened Wood Jack was,
    Beside a trickling stream,
Snatched from Abaddon's hungry jaws,
    The Tower but a dream.

XVIII.
Hexana

Hexana was a sorceress,
    Or Hecate her name;
Pale white her skin and black her dress—
    Methinks them both the same.

She dwelt deep in the forest's reach,
    Where valiance may pall,
And oftentimes an owl's harsh screech
    Will mark a hero's fall.

She made her home in ruins, cold,
    A tower, fallen, stone,
A prison where, in days of old,
    A princess wept, alone.

Hexana owned a silver glass
    That whispered monstrous lies;
Her wickedness none dared surpass,
    And from the forest, cries.

At Yuletide on the longest night
    Hexana danced alone,
Her naked skin bathed in the light
    The moon upon her shone.

XVIII. Hexana

She danced within a ring of stones,
    Much blood upon them spilled;
And with ecstatic keens and moans
    The empty night was filled.

She summoned forth her dark desire,
    Which welled from depths of black;
It filled her soul with urgent fire,
    Her will to conquer Jack.

It only took a day before
    Her scarlet wish came true;
Jack knocked three times upon her door,
    His feather'd hat askew.

The sorceress asked Jack to dine,
    To sample of her meat;
Blood-red her lips, like vintage wine,
    Her breath was hot and sweet.

They tussled long upon her bed,
    The mirror on the wall;
The blazing fire, orange and red,
    At last began to pall.

XVIII. HEXANA

Hexana fell in slumber's thrall,
    Though Jack stayed wide awake,
And in the mirror on the wall
    A sight caused him to quake.

A withered hag lay next to him,
    And not a tender maid;
He grabbed his sword upon a whim—
    His undefeated blade.

A thought right then occurred to Jack,
    Whose artifice was keen;
He swung the hilt and made a crack
    Upon the mirror's sheen.

And in a trice the mirror broke
    And set the Elf-King free,
His visage laughing in the smoke,
    A dæmon filled with glee.

Jack spared a glance to-wards the bed:
    His lover now was dust;
Then from the tower fast he fled—
    Stone-cold Hexana's lust.

XIX.
Yᵉ Historie
of
Jack o' Lanthorne,
or,
The Devil's Spark

*

*

* * *

*

A Play for Marionettes

*** Dramatis Personae ***

JACK, an artful drunkard
SCRATCH, a kingly nicknevin
OBADIAH, a sardonic innkeeper
EZEKIEL, a recording angel

The Time: The Days of Yore
The Place: Yᵉ Toad and Crow, The Cross-roads, The Gates of Heaven,
The Gates of Hell

* * * *

A Fiend's Glossary

Clabbernap. A supernatural creature vaguely described in Cornish lore. So called because of the ringing sound it makes at night, like the clapper of a bell.

Clurican. An Irish variety of pixie. Said to be a drunkard, though this is probably scurrilous.

Hallow-tide. The witch-haunted night preceding All Hallows' Day. Otherwise known as Samhain.

Harpy. A shrill shrieking spectre, like a wife who won't leave you alone until you've finished fixing the roof.

Hell-wain. A demonic carriage pulled by six black horses and driven by a skeletal wraith. It is waiting for you outside.

Hobhoulard. Yet another of the plethoric family of fae folk. Second cousin to a robin-goodfellow and great-nephew to a brownie.

Imp. A hopping spriggan. A jack-be-nimble. A jumping-joan.

Mawkin. A scarecrow or simpleton in the Scots dialect. Also a hare.

Mendicant. A beggar. A tom-o'-bedlam. One who wanders abroad at night singing for his supper. Probably quite mad. Can also refer to one who practises the vulgar American custom of 'trick-or-treating.'

Nicknevin. A daughter of Scáthach, the Queen of Faerie. Or a son of Old Nick. I'm not sure which.

Shellycoat. A water sprite, given this name due to the assortment of shells adorning its coat.

ACT ONE

Scene: Y^e Toad and Crow, a tavern in Old Hexham Town.

Enter OBADIAH. Enter JACK.

JACK: Good Hallow's Eve, my dear old friend—
Pray pour me out a drink!
The darkened moon and stars portend
An eldritch night, I think.

OBADIAH: Thou art an utter madman, Jack,
To think I'd pour for you—
A man whose soul is pitchest black
And never speaketh true.

JACK: You wound me, sir, right to the quick;
Your words are sharp and steel!
Now if it's not impolitic,
A burning thirst I feel . . .

OBADIAH: Oh, save your breath, you drunken sot;
Your debt is long past due.
Unless a coin of gold you've got,
Your drinking days are through.

Exit OBADIAH. Enter SCRATCH.

SCRATCH: Good eventide, my gentle Jack—
I see we are well met:
A fellow pilgrim on the track,
With muddy boots and wet.

My name is Scratch, an ancient line:
I introduce myself,
A nicknevin some will opine,
A species of black elf.

[68]

I offer you a chosen boon
And name my price your soul;
This Hallow-tide I see the moon
Is new and black as coal.

JACK: Thou art an imp, good Master Scratch,
A hobhoulard, for sure.
Well, I can see I've met my match;
I can't resist your lure.

If you can turn into a coin
So I may buy a drink,
Then I shall do as you enjoin
And spill my blood for ink.

SCRATCH: A simple trick for me to do:
Behold a coin of gold!

Raise SCRATCH offstage.

* LOWER COIN AND HOLD IN MIDAIR. *

JACK: Well, I'll be damned; he's spoken true.
I fear my soul is sold!
Unless . . .

JACK snatches the coin from the air and puts it in his pocket.

* HIDE COIN BEHIND JACK. *

SCRATCH: (voice offstage) Now I object, good sir!
What have you done?
This immuration I demur;
I seek you quit this fun.

JACK: Inside my pocket is a cross;
You fell into my snare!

| | Well, is your wit now at a loss? |
| | What do you say in there? |

| SCRATCH: | O, let me out! Release me now! |
| | Pray, what is your demand? |

JACK:	Quite simple, sir, you wirrikow,
	Whose hide I just have tanned.
	For twenty years now leave me be,
	And then my soul I'll yield;
	I'll meet you by the apple tree
	That grows in Whateley's Field.

| SCRATCH: | These terms I must agree to Jack; |
| | Release me now, I pray. |

* RAISE COIN PROP OFFSTAGE. *

Lower SCRATCH back onto the stage.

| SCRATCH: | We'll meet upon the Ancient Track, |
| | Come twenty years to-day! |

Exit Scratch.

* * * Close curtain. * * *

ACT TWO

Scene: Whateley's Field. A thorny heath where a gnarled old tree grows with a single red apple.

Enter JACK. Enter SCRATCH.

SCRATCH:	You thought that you were rid of me,
	But I just had to wait;
	For such a man as lazy Jack

Cannot outrun his fate.

JACK: Well, I declare, good Master Scratch,
I see I'm just in time;
In artfulness I've met my match—
I must be past my prime.

But would you do one thing for me,
For poor defeated Jack?
Would you climb up this apple tree
And fetch me down a snack?

SCRATCH: Why, nothing else would please me more
Than that I grant this gift;
For me it is a trifling chore—
Do help me with a lift.

JACK helps SCRATCH up the apple tree. SCRATCH climbs up to one of the braches and reaches for an apple. In the meantime, JACK places a cross at the base of the tree.

* LOWER CROSS AND SET AT BASE OF TREE. *

SCRATCH: What have you done, you blasted cheat?
Your cross traps me up here!

JACK: Oh, listen to him bray and bleat,
The whining puppeteer!

This hell-wain is an easy mark;
I've plucked him like a goose.
Well, this is such a merry lark;
Why should I turn him loose?

SCRATCH: O, Master Jack! The day is won;
I'm beaten; I concede.

| | I fold my hand, the deal is done; |
| | Now let me down, I plead. |

JACK: Be quiet now, you clabbernap,
And I'll strike you a deal:
If I release you from this trap,
My soul you must not steal.

SCRATCH: It seems I'm left without a choice;
I'm bested by your wit;
Without a doubt you will rejoice;
My failing I admit.

I make a vow right here to haunt
You for your soul no more;
But you in turn must never flaunt
This triumph, I implore.

JACK: Why, Master Scratch, you clurican—
You only had to ask.
And now we've settled, man to man,
I shall fulfill my task.

* RAISE CROSS OFFSTAGE. *

SCRATCH climbs down from the apple tree.

SCRATCH: And so, good sir, I call us quits;
I bid thee now farewell.
Our path from here in two forks splits,
And mine goes back to Hell.

Exit SCRATCH. Exit JACK.

* * * Close curtain * * *

ACT THREE

Scene: The Gates of Heaven. In front of the gate is a lectern and atop the lectern is Yᴱ Bᴜᴋᴇ ᴏғ Tɪᴍᴇ. Eᴢᴇᴋɪᴇʟ, a recording angel, is standing behind the lectern.

EZEKIEL: In course of time men turn to dust,
             And then they must be judged;
             God's will is harsh, mayhap, but just,
             For truth cannot be fudged.

Enter JACK.

JACK: Good day to you; my name is Jack,
             And I have fallen dead;
             So long I've trod the lonesome track,
             No tears for me were shed.

EZEKIEL: Ezekiel to all I'm known,
             And I am heaven's clerk,
             Admitting those who've goodness shown—
             The rest consigned to dark.

JACK: And who are you to judge me so?
             To call me bad or good?
             My heart no other man can know,
             My deeds misunderstood.

EZEKIEL: Not I, but God, who knows all things,
             And writes them in His Buke,
             So when Grim Death a harvest brings,
             I open it to look.

JACK: Well, open up your book and see
             If Jack therein is writ,
             And if you do, you must agree
             That God condones my wit.

Ezekiel examines Yᵉ Buke.

EZEKIEL: Hmmm . . . Jack, you say? Then I shall look
            Inside my hallowed tome,
            For on the pages of this book
            All Time doth find a home.

            I see Jack Baker; is that you?

JACK: Good grain makes better beer.

EZEKIEL: Hmmm . . . Jack of Hearts, the lover true?

JACK: I never was, I fear.

EZEKIEL: Jack Horner, Straw, One-eyed, or Sprat?

JACK: Alas, these are not me.

EZEKIEL: Then, sir, I must acknowledge that
            Your name I do not see.

JACK: What does this mean? That I am doomed?
            Cast out to burn in Hell?
            My soul in dancing fire consumed
            Eternally to dwell?

EZEKIEL: 'Tis true, dear sir, thou banished art,
            Like Lucifer who fell;
            No craft can hide what's in thy heart:
            A black one bound for Hell.

JACK: So be it then; the die is tossed;
            I must accept my fate.
            To Satan's kingdom I am lost,
            And barred is Heaven's gate.

            * * * Close curtain * * *

ACT FOUR

Scene: The Gates of Hell, a fearful place. A mawkin yowls and hisses. A harpy shrieks.

Enter JACK.

JACK: And so I reach the Gates of Hell:
          A sordid, dismal fate;
          O, is that sulphur that I smell?
          What tortures me await?

Enter SCRATCH.

SCRATCH: We meet again, my gentle Jack;
          Our stars must be aligned.
          I thought we'd parted on the track
          A thousand leagues behind.

JACK: And so did I, you shellycoat;
          I thought I'd beaten you,
          For though you'd sworn me not to gloat,
          I knew it to be true.

SCRATCH: Then why did you come to my door,
          And loudly on it knock?
          I thought I caused you to deplore,
          To jest and jeer and mock?

JACK: My mortal life has reached its end,
          And Heaven's cast me off.
          I thought in Hell I'd find a friend,
          And so my hat I doff.

JACK bows.

SCRATCH: The tide has turned, O Stingy Jack,
          A mendicant, I think;

So hat in hand you have come back?
I laugh! I'm tickled pink!

Alas, I must refuse your plea
To enter in Hell's gate,
For once you forced a vow from me:
Your soul to abrogate.

JACK: But Master Scratch, what is my fate?
I'm racked with fear and doubt;
For Heaven's turned me from its gate,
And Hell has cast me out.

SCRATCH: Into the darkness you must go
To wander evermore,
Until Time's sands no longer flow
You'll make your weary tour.

But since I'm kind, I'll do a turn
For you, my kinsman Jack:
With hell-fire will this lanthorn burn,
And light your Ancient Track.

* LOWER LANTHORN. *

JACK: Then Jack o' Lanthorn shall I be;
At night I'll haunt the reed,
And if my wispy light you see,
In it your ruin's seed.

* * * Close curtain * * *

THE END

*

*

* * *

*

[76]

XX.
Crimson Jack

He called upon Walpurgis Night,
      The man called Crimson Jack,
A dæmon-lanthorn casting light
      Upon his ancient track,

A-wandering a thousand years;
      Jack's story now I'll tell:
Expelled from heaven's glowing spheres
      And banished from dark Hell.

Now, once a hundred years or so,
      He visited an inn,
The Toad and Crow as some may know,
      A site of secret sin.

This creaking house had many rooms,
      And also many doors;
Behind them men have met their dooms
      By listening to whores.

Well, Jack was ardent for a drink;
      His road was long and dry;
His face was handsome and his wink
      Caused many girls to sigh.

XX. Crimson Jack

'An ale,' he called. 'To ease my thirst.'
　　The alewife pursed her lips.
'I'll draw you one if you can first
　　Appease what's in my hips.'

Jack's mouth contorted in a grin.
　　'I like my women raw!
To-night let's try to glut what's in
　　Your all-consuming maw.'

Jack set his lanthorn on the bar
　　And drank his hard-won ale;
The man beside, as black as tar,
　　Asked if it were for sale.

'Why, this old thing?' Jack played it coy.
　　'This battered hunk of tin,
Not even fit to be a toy—
　　Who knows where it has been?'

Well, this was not just any lamp—
　　Its embers borne from Hell;
No gust of wind or winter's damp
　　Its light could ever quell.

XX. Crimson Jack

'What say I offer you a thing,
  The treasure of a life:
This rune-engraven golden ring
  Which binds a pixie-wife?'

Well, Jack was wily, Jack was sly,
  Proposing then a game:
To catch the other in a lie
  And then both prizes claim.

They flipped a coin for who went first,
  With Jack of course in luck;
For though by Satan he was cursed,
  His fortune ran amok.

'My next words are the truth,' he said.
  'My last words were a lie.'
The Black Man, reeling, clutched his head
  And from the inn did fly.

Jack took the ring up to a room
  To see what it could do,
And like a flower's petals bloom
  A pixie from it grew.

XX. Crimson Jack

'I am your wife,' she said to him.
　　'What would you have of me?'
And though it may have been a whim,
　　Jack thought to set her free.

The pixie kissed his lips in joy
　　And said she owed her life.
'Just call me if you want me, boy,
　　For I am still your wife.'

And then she flew into the night,
　　Though Jack was not alone;
For in the lanthorn's dæmon-light
　　A lover's body shone.

XXI.
Hellbound Jack

The Scarlet Balladress came to a crossroads in the middle of nowhere. It was a hot evening in late August, and her feet were sore from walking. She sat beneath the shade of an old willow tree and listened to the cicadas whine. She knew the Devil was close.

She laid her black guitar across her lap and strummed a mournful tune that she'd learned from a witch, then let it die away. Before long she heard a rustling in the thorn. The air smelled metallic, as it did before a thunderstorm. A man appeared before her. He was naked, and his skin and hair—everything about him—was as black as tar. In place of feet he had hooves, and on his head were two horns, as sharp as knives.

"Play me a song, Balladress," he said to her, his voice tolling like a bell. "Play me a song about Jack." She smiled, for nothing gave her greater pleasure. Her soul and Jack's were conjoined, as surely as if they were married, though he would always wander free, and so would she. Night came to the holler, and her song echoed around the mountains long after she had gone.

> My name is Jack; you've heard of me,
>> For I have plundered Hell,
> Where I made Satan bend a knee
>> To me, the Ettinfell.
>
> When I was seven years of age,
>> O'er oxen I stood guard.
> A parson came, his manner sage;
>> His shepherd's crook was hard.

XXI. Hellbound Jack

'Of God's commandments there are ten,'
        With lofty airs he said;
I quipped, 'But only nine ones when
        You took your maid a-bed.'

I laughed at his discomfort now,
        And asked of him to say
Who made these oxen, knowing how
        Much like an ass he'd bray.

'Why, God above did make them, Jack,'
        He said, his finger raised.
To think I should this knowledge lack
        Did leave him much amazed.

I cocked a smile and said, 'Why no,
        God made them each a bull.
My father made them oxen so
        They would his plough a-pull.'

'Thou art a wag!' the parson cried,
        And fled then far away—
A fact I never have denied,
        Not even to this day.

XXI. Hellbound Jack

You may have heard a tale or two
    Told of my tricksome ways;
Though oft in doubt if they are true,
    My stories much amaze.

You must have heard the tale of how
    I felled old Cormoran,
Who was a giant I avow,
    Full eighteen feet in span.

Before his keep I dug a pit
    And covered it with sticks;
As always I employed my wit
    And won the day with tricks.

When stirred the dawn, I loudly blew
    Tantivy on my horn,
And like a strutting cock I crew
    The advent of the morn.

The giant came a-stumbling from
    His dank and fœtid lair;
It caused my heart to madly thrum
    And prickled up my hair.

XXI. HELLBOUND JACK

'How dare that you disturb my sleep!'
 The giant loudly yelled,
Before he tumbled in so deep,
 He was then all but felled.

'Into Lob's Pound hast thou got down,'
 I taunted thus my foe
Before my pickaxe met his crown
 And caused his brains to flow.

And other giants then I slew,
 In England and in Wales;
My fame for felling ettins grew,
 Immortal are my tales.

Just how they came that way is black:
 The Devil's work it was;
But because my name is Jack,
 I found a get-out clause.

The tale of how I worked this deal
 Has never ere been told,
And how I made the Devil kneel,
 A sight shall few behold.

XXI. HELLBOUND JACK

It started in a market square,
    Where I a taint beheld:
A funeral impeded there,
    A sight unparalleled.

The mourners laid the coffin down,
    Inside a man in debt;
He owed vast sums to those in town,
    A fact none could forget.

A noble prince, King Arthur's son
    Repaid each one his due,
Until at last the deal was done;
    The dead could now pass through.

This act of generosity
    Stirred something in my soul;
My canny virtuosity
    I pledged to serve his goal.

A reckoning for being freed,
    His angel now I was;
The dead was grateful for the deed
    And followed ancient laws.

XXI. Hellbound Jack

Deep in the dark wood's mazy thorn
    A lady lay enthralled;
To rescue her the prince had sworn,
    To her his heart was called.

But now he had not any gold
    To lodge us in a room;
We shivered greatly from the cold
    As gathered fast the gloom.

But I was not in need of wit
    To quickly form a scheme;
Into the darkened wood we lit,
    And crossed then into Dreame.

It was not very far away
    That in a castle dwelled
My uncle who was, sad to say,
    An ettin left unfelled.

I bade the prince to hide in thorn
    While I called on my kin;
I told him that I'd blow my horn
    To call him safely in.

XXI. Hellbound Jack

'O, who is there?' the giant boomed.
I answered, 'I am Jack.
I've come to warn thee thou art doomed;
'Tis heavy news, alack!'

The giant's laughter shook the earth;
'Why, surely thou must jest.
This claim thou makest brings me mirth
Of which I'm seldom blest.

'An ettin earl with heads of three,
I have but little fear;
Five hundred men could not kill me,
Nor even come they near.'

'Aha!' I said. 'But Arthur's son
Has got a thousand men;
And when they come your days are done,
For they will kill you then.'

'O, Jack!' he cried, my ettin kin,
'Then I must hide away!
Although it causes me chagrin,
I shall not be their prey.'

XXI. Hellbound Jack

I locked the giant in a vault
    And turned the iron key.
Well, is it truly all my fault
    This fool so trusted me?

The giant safely all locked up,
    I sounded loud my horn
To call my master in to sup
    From hiding in the thorn.

We rattled all the dishes well
    And made an awful sound
To scare the giant in his hell
    Deep underneath the ground.

And after we had fed and slept,
    My master left to hide;
I opened up the vault that kept
    The ettin safe inside.

'O, bless you, Jack,' my uncle cried.
    'I owe you now my life;
I tell you true I would have died
    If I had faced such strife.

XXI. Hellbound Jack

'I beg to offer you a prize
        What e'er your eyes may see;
For saving me from my demise
        Take what you want from me.'

'Four things there are beside your bed:
        A cap and coat and shoes,
And rusty sword,' to him I said.
        'These are the gifts I choose.'

'O, they will serve you very well,'
        The ettin said to me.
'For with them you may harrow Hell
        And climb the Devil's tree.

'The cap is charmed to know all things;
        The coat keeps you unseen;
The shoes will give you angel's wings;
        The sword is dæmon-keen.

'I offer them with all my heart
        To you, my kindred Jack;
The deal is done so we may part
        And never come you back.'

XXI. Hellbound Jack

I found myself then eldritch-armed
  And joined my gentle prince;
My trickery left him alarmed,
  Its telling made him wince.

We set off deeper in the wood,
  And came soon to the end;
I told the prince that I was good,
  To count me as a friend.

I wondered though deep in my heart
  If good is what I was;
For when I practiced cunning art
  Was it for noble cause?

An ancient castle by us loomed;
  The lady let us in,
Her hair in raven whorls, perfumed;
  Upon her face, a grin.

She led us to her hall to dine,
  The prince there made his suit;
Her mermaid eyes caused him to pine,
  Her lips like luscious fruit.

XXI. Hellbound Jack

And at the lavish banquet's end
  She took a handkerchief
To wipe the mouth of my dear friend,
  Now slack with disbelief.

'Do furnish me this cloth come morn,'
  The lady mordant said.
'And then to you my hand is sworn,
  Or else it means your head.'

The prince in sorrow went a-bed,
  But I was still his Jack;
My Know-All cap upon my head,
  I peered into the black.

I learnt the lady read a book,
  A grimoire stained and old,
Which caused her will to be forsook,
  By Lucifer controlled.

Hid by my coat, I watched her chant
  And open up a door,
Which access into Hell would grant
  By stairs below the floor.

XXI. Hellbound Jack

I overtook her long descent,
    My shoes providing haste;
And when I saw just where she went
    My heart as quickly raced.

I passed through spheres in number nine,
    The blackened shucks of Hell;
The horrors in them chilled my spine
    As through their midst I fell.

At last I reached the lowest sphere,
    Where Lucifer held court;
I strained myself to overhear
    The witch's hushed report.

She handed him the handkerchief,
    Still stained from princely lips;
Her merriment beyond belief,
    To Satan she made quips!

The Devil laid it on a shelf,
    Which I stole then in stealth;
Quite rightly I applaud myself
    For bolting with my health.

XXI. HELLBOUND JACK

The prince come morning gave his weel
    The cloth I took from Hell,
Which I had fled on wingèd feet
    And lived the tale to tell.

That night the lady laid a spread
    And made another threat:
The prince would lose his precious head
    Unless he won her bet.

'Come dawn I charge you show the mouth
    That this night has kissed mine,
And if this trial brings you drouth
    Pray drink deep of the wine.'

'But if he does,' I challenged her.
    'Then you must be his wife.'
And though she hemmed and made demur,
    She pledged upon her life.

Well, as she had the night before,
    The lady read her book—
That fiendish store of crimson lore,
    A cruel black shepherd's crook.

XXI. Hellbound Jack

I followed her wrapped in my coat,
  Which made my sight unseen,
And watched her kiss that hoary goat,
  Majestic in his mien.

When she was gone, the Devil laughed
  And claimed I was revealed,
For he could smell the wizard-craft
  That kept my form concealed.

I gambled that it was a bluff
  That he in truth could see,
And tossed a copper coin, enough
  To make him bend a knee.

Then drawing fast my eldritch sword,
  I cut off Satan's head;
Well, you will have to take my word
  The truth of what I've said.

And come the morn, my master laid
  That head upon a board;
The Devil's debt had now been paid—
  The prince took his reward.

XXI. Hellbound Jack

And for my service in this task
King Arthur dubbed me Sir;
I kept my face aloof, a mask,
Though pride it did bestir.

The Balladress awoke at daybreak and shivered in her scarlet cloak, besodden with dew. Her guitar lay on the ground beside her. The man was gone, but the metallic smell still lingered in the air. She took up the guitar and started down the road once more. The deal was done. Her soul and Jack's were one.

XXII.
The Samhanach

Into the land of dreams Jack goes;
    When he returns nobody knows,
Till far away his slug-horn blows,
    And then the wine of story flows.

The giant-killer he is called,
    This gallant Ettinfell,
Whose stories keep the mind enthralled,
    Should any care to tell.

On Hallow's Eve the Balladress
    Stopped by the Toad and Crow;
They knew her by her scarlet dress,
    Her skin as white as snow.

Her tresses are so raven black,
    And mournful how she sings,
And in the fire dances Jack
    When she a-strums her strings.

Hear: Jack was wand'ring in the Wood
    Upon the Ancient Track;
He wandered farther than is good
    And never once looked back.

XXII. THE SAMHANACH

He fared beyond the Elf-Queen's bourn
    Into the northern waste,
Where nothing grows but prickly thorn,
    And horrors must be faced.

The Samhanach was lurking there
    And in a castle dwelt;
His tooth and nail brought children fear,
    Their skin made him a pelt.

When Jack came to the castle's gate
    He blew upon his horn,
And trusted to the lucky fate
    He'd had since he was born.

The Samhanach invited Jack
    To dine within his hall,
A respite from the Ancient Track,
    Which had begun to pall.

The Samhanach began to jest
    That Jack was lacking size;
Jack asked his host to pose a test
    And not to criticise.

XXII. THE SAMHANACH

Jack quoth that he could quicker eat
    The contents of the feast,
And bragged that he could not be beat
    By Ettin, man, or beast.

He shovelled food into a sack
    Near infinite within
An old man once had given Jack—
    But then he lost his grin . . .

The Samhanach ate cups and chairs,
    The table in one chew;
'So loses anyone who dares
    To challenge me!' he crew.

The glutted giant fell asleep,
    And Jack his sword then drew
To slice the ettin's neck so deep
    His head would fall askew.

The sword was charmed to be so sharp
    That it could never fail;
The giant only woke to carp
    A rat had thrashed its tail.

XXII. The Samhanach

The ettin called his beldam to
    Play Jack a betting game;
Jack's luck of course as all men knew
    Had brought abundant fame.

But though the game was very close,
    Jack had to fold his hand;
Of stark defeat he had a dose—
    His hide had been well tanned.

Then dawn arose and Jack set out
    To leave this ettin's hall:
The only giant who could flout
    Jack's skill to bring a fall.

The Samhanach outside then crew
    To Jack of his deceit;
A revelation now was due
    Explaining Jack's defeat.

'It was not I who ate the feast,
    But blazing fire itself;
None could have beat it, not a beast
    Or man or god or elf.

XXII. The Samhanach

'You did not cut my neck last night:
    Instead a mountain-top,
And carved a valley with the might
    Of that titanic chop.

'The woman you played poker with:
    Incarnate Lady Luck;
Fortuna she is known in myth—
    With you she runs a-muck.'

And then the castle disappeared,
    The Samhanach as well;
Jack never had been so a-feared
    Since journeying to Hell.

The Balladress then quit her song
    And quieted her strings;
The tune however lingered long,
    A dream on timeless wings.

And at the door a man came in:
    It was bedraggled Jack,
All tattertorn and deathly thin,
    From Thule just come back.

XXII. THE SAMHANACH

He took the Balladress's hand
    And led her up the stair;
This moment surely Fate had planned,
    This overdue affair.

XXIII.
The Hidden Door

When Jack was forty-six years old
    He found a silver key,
Which once was lost as has been told
    By better bards than me.

He found it in a cedar box
    Upon a velvet bed,
When three was chiming all the clocks
    To echo in his head.

Well, he was only seven when
    He found the hidden door
That opened wide admitting then
    This boy to lands of yore.

He wandered far upon the track
    And outguessed many foes
To win the fame of gallant Jack,
    Whose glory ever grows.

All this he did before the clocks
    Were finished striking three;
And back into the cedar box
    Jack put the silver key.

XXIII. THE HIDDEN DOOR

He did not find this key again
    Until his grandma died;
His age was twenty-three years then,
    His character untried.

Jack lived atop a noble hill,
    A Drake of Boston Town,
And to this day he lives there still,
    Though shuns his great renown.

The silver key takes many shapes,
    Addictive are they all;
Who uses it the world escapes,
    Which brings about a fall.

The second time Jack saw the door,
    The key a powder was,
Which made him sick upon the floor,
    And then into a vase.

Jack Drake became a Jack of Spades,
    A needle for a sword;
In dreams this keenest honed of blades
    Made Jack a one-man horde.

XXIII. THE HIDDEN DOOR

From Gandermoon to Hexham Town
    Jack wandered far and wide;
His exploits brought him much renown,
    Which was a source of pride.

But always then he would awake
    To find himself in bed,
And nothing could appease the ache
    That throbbed inside his head.

He dwelt upon a tune he'd heard
    Deep in the darkest wood;
The passion in him that it spurred
    He never understood.

A woman strummed, a balladress,
    Whose strings were silver, strange;
Her tangled hair her only dress,
    Her voice of ghostly range.

They coupled there beside the stream,
    Where rowed a haunted boat
That carried souls to death from dream
    To face a hornèd goat.

XXIII. THE HIDDEN DOOR

And from their union sprang a son,
  Who bore the blood of Drake;
This memory Jack came to shun
  When he was wide awake.

But when he came to middle age,
  Jack knew he must return
Before he left the worldly stage,
  For ballads made him yearn.

And so he found the silver key
  Inside its cedar box;
The door he found inside a tree,
  When three chimed all the clocks.

He found himself upon the track
  That he had trod in youth;
In dreams he felt much more like Jack,
  Which pleased him well in truth.

He felt again like twenty-three,
  His wit was bright and keen;
Such was the power of the key
  For dreams were ever green.

XXIII. THE HIDDEN DOOR

The ancient track then crossed a road,
    A tavern crouching there;
Nearby a narrow stream a-flowed,
    Across which hopped a hare.

Jack entered in the Toad and Crow,
    As once he had before;
The barman seemed his face to know
    And for him 'gan to pour.

The Balladress was in there too,
    And played for Jack a tune;
Their separation brought him rue—
    That night beneath the moon.

The Balladress was older now,
    And played for Jack a song;
But shedding tears she'd not allow,
    Although she'd waited long.

Jack climbed a tower every night,
    Which kept atop a maid
With lips blood red and skin snow white,
    Although he never stayed.

XXIII. THE HIDDEN DOOR

He climbed a ladder of her hair,
    A beanstalk spun from gold,
To look upon a face so fair
    A thousand tales were told.

Her mistress was a sorceress
    Who knew of Jack's coy game:
So sang the wistful balladress,
    Whose hair she could not tame.

The evil witch then cast her out
    And waited for Jack's climb;
His cunning tricks she aimed to rout
    And punish in due time.

The crone threw Jack into the thorn,
    Which scratched out both his eyes,
And then he wandered lost, forlorn,
    A beggar now his guise.

When years had passed he found a shack
    Deep in the tangled wood;
The balladress admitted Jack,
    Who learned his fatherhood.

XXIII. THE HIDDEN DOOR

Her tears of joy restored his eyes,
    And then Jack glimpsed his son,
A boy of seven—how time flies!—
    This triumph he had won.

But then Jack blinked; the door shut fast,
    And lost the silver key;
That glimpse he knew would be his last,
    And sorrowful was he.

XXIV.
Cruel Eleanora

Once Eleanora schemed to wed
    Her sister's suitor Jack,
And sent her to a river bed
    To end her life, alack.

But on the wedding day there came
    A wayward balladeer,
Whose ballads garnered spreading fame
    That rumoured him a seer.

He had a harp of bones he made
    From Elspeth's grim remains,
Which in the river had decayed,
    For time our flesh disdains.

This harp was haunted and decried
    Her murder, drowned and cold;
Then all there knew how Elspeth died:
    A dismal story told.

Cruel Eleanora fled from there
    In shame and in disgrace;
A streak ran through her raven hair,
    And malice marked her face.

XXIV. CRUEL ELEANORA

A sorceress she now became
 And dwelt in tangled thorn;
Her wickedness brought her dark fame,
 Yet still she was forlorn.

She learned about the Ballad Stone,
 A sapphire steeped in doom,
And vowed to make it hers alone,
 A jewel to suit her gloom.

She sent an owl, its talons sharp,
 To soar across Lake Nod,
To where the Duke a-played his harp
 With no one to applaud.

And when the Duke fell fast asleep
 On ballads drunk and wine,
The stone was stolen from his keep,
 A master-stroke malign.

The Duke of Ballads then awoke
 To find his treasure gone,
And tears his silk cravat would soak
 As broke the hated dawn.

XXV.
Red Jack

A phantom haunted London Town—
    The shadows whispered Jack;
He stalked the girls in scarlet gown,
    Whose eyes were cold and black.

The Devil some believed he was,
    A fiend from darkest Hell;
The things he did no Christian does,
    Disquieting to tell.

His lanthorn flickered in the night,
    A dancing demon spark
To mesmerise who saw its light,
    And lead them through the dark,

Through alleys foul to rooms unclean
    To satisfy Jack's need,
A scarlet horror later seen
    To evidence the deed.

Some said Jack wore a high silk hat,
    Some said his style was old;
In truth he left none living that
    These details could have told.

XXV. RED JACK

Red Jack! Red Jack! all London screamed;
    The church bells tolled his name,
And red with blood the gutters streamed
    To Scotland Yard's great shame.

Five harlots fell to Jack's keen knife:
    Two Marys, Anne, and Bess,
And Catherine who lost her life,
    Her kidney too no less.

Then like the fog Jack swirled away,
    His lanthorn seen no more;
Though afterwards 'twas shunned to say
    His name by any whore.

XXVI.
The Witch's Son

There was a witch called Betty Crow
    Who had a son named Jack;
The thing about them both, you know:
    Their hearts were cruel and black.

Their hearts was black as were their souls,
    For they were devil's kin;
And for these two no church bell tolls,
    Their lives immersed in sin.

At night the graveyard they would haunt,
    A mother and her son,
Where they their wickedness could flaunt,
    Their wrongs espied by none

But owls who perched in bare-branched trees
    And by the silver moon,
While whistled by a chilling breeze,
    For winter's time was soon.

And of their rites I dare not speak:
    They summoned things below
By speaking Latin, and in Greek,
    Which both of them did know.

XXVI. The Witch's Son

In course of years old Betty died,

But Jack is still alive,

And if in you I may confide:

Her corpse he yet may swive.

XXVII.
The Lay of Dumah

Lazarus Craven nursed a secret passion for the grave. In the dead of night he would steal from his ramshackle palisade of wormy clapboards and rusty nails, and visit the graveyard at the edge of town. Eschewing the company of his living neighbours, he preferred instead to call upon his familiar crypts and gravestones, where he would drink cup after cup of wormwood tea. Under a willow tree lay his favourite grave, which bore an unpolished stone in which was lovingly chiselled the single name MARY. No family name, no dates; just Mary. The stone was the colour of rose: a gentle pink by day, flushing blood-red at night.

Lazarus's love for Mary grew stronger with each visit. In time he spent all his nights with her, curling up to her stone to feel the seeping warmth she had patiently gathered for him during the day. He rarely went out into the light anymore; his skin was pale and drawn, his teeth sharp and pointed like a rat's from eating dry crusts of bread. The pleasures of life no longer gave him joy, only his love for Mary. But as the days of autumn grew shorter, the stone grew ever colder when what he craved was warmth.

Lazarus's craving was felt by Dumah in the nethermost pit of the Deep, Dumah the Lord of Putrefaction and Decay, who said unto him: *Get thee thy spade and shovel.* So the next night Lazarus got him his spade and shovel, and dug into the worm-crawling earth. He dug through the gnarl-creeping roots of the willow tree until the iron tip of his shovel struck solid oak, a coffin carved with the lonely letter 'M.' And Dumah said unto him: *Get thee thy hammer and crowbar.* So Lazarus returned the next night with his hammer and crowbar, and prised open the coffin to behold an ivory-skinned maiden set like a jewel upon a shimmering bed of ruby-red velvet. And Dumah said: *Get thee thy sickle and scythe.*

The next night the wolf-wind howled and tore at his flesh with icy claws when Lazarus came to reap his bloody harvest. He lay down in the open grave taking his unnatural pleasures with his dæmon-bride until the robin chirped the first stirrings of dawn, when he scurried back to his hole to await the coming of night. His unspeakable passion grew stronger as the nights grew longer, and the white blanket of snow that settled over the ground only kindled his craving for Mary, whose bosom swelled with warmth as the winter wore on.

But he found his own body was growing colder; his skin was icy to the touch, and he could no longer feel his fingers and toes. Then, one night in the dead of winter, the cock crowed the dawn, and he could not summon the strength to rise from his embrace with Mary, whose lips twisted into a cruel smile as she rose from the grave and, with his own shovel, buried Lazarus Craven's lifeless body beneath the cold earth.

> *Dumah lies*
> *Beneath the ground,*
> *Telling lies*
> *Without a sound.*

XXVIII.
Mary of the Rosy Grave

by K. A. Opperman

Mary 'neath the weeping willow,
Mary of the rosy grave,
I would make for me a pillow
'Mid your bosom's ivory nave.

Mary in your ruby bedding,
Mary like a moon-white gem,
Soon shall be our blessèd wedding,
Mushroom-ring our diadem.

Mary, dead and yet undying,
Mary, uncorrupt of rot,
I have heard you softly sighing
In your warm and perfumed plot.

Mary, I have heard the demon;
Mary, does he tell me lies?
Mary, make of me your leman—
Mary, drink my soul and rise.

—After "The Lay of Dumah," by Adam Bolivar

XXIX.
The Black Shepherd

The white shepherd tends his flock
With a curling crosier to keep
Mindful of the thoughts
Of each and every sheep,

Until the tender lamb
Strayed from his master's gaze,
Seeking grass in greener land
To sate his lustful graze.

Far from the comfort of the fold,
The hunger took its toll;
The winding heath was stark and cold,
And the lone wolf preyed upon his soul.

The worms well feasted on his flesh,
And the crows did pick his eyes;
For alas his ears were deaf
To all good shepherd's cries.

XXIX. THE BLACK SHEPHERD

So may these words serve as warning
To all who feel the hungry yearning
To flee white shepherd and his flock
And seek the comfort of the black
At the peril of your bones and blood;

For his winding crook will only fit
The ones possessed of keenest wit.

XXX.
A Page from Jack's Diary

I sing the Lady Ashiel,
    Whose witchcraft none could quell,
Who in the gloom of Night would dwell
    To conjure fiends from Hell.

I wandered far across the land
    And always heard the same:
From ice of north to southern sand
    Is feared this lady's name.

And so into the waste I struck
    To find the Sorceress,
And though I knew I pushed my luck,
    I frankly must confess

That more than e'en her dæmon ways,
    Her pulchritude was told,
And for a sight I trudged for days,
    That fairness to behold.

At last I came where once she dwelt,
    A ruin, black and cold,
And there before a grave I knelt:
    Rain-worn and very old.

XXX. A Page from Jack's Diary

Embracing it with prickly thorn,
A crimson rose there grew;
The Lady's lover bode forlorn—
I wept for love so true.

XXXI.
The Silver Gate

Jack entered into Faerie-Land,
    Which hath a silver gate;
He opened it with trembling hand,
    Uncertain of his fate.

The Queen of Faerie met him there,
    Suffused in silver light;
Beside her was a rampant hare
    Who tempted Jack to flight,

And led him to a secret pool
    With waters weird and black;
Who drank of them would be a fool,
    But such a fool was Jack.

He sipped a potion poisoned by
    A gnarled tree's eldritch sap,
And in a trance he could descry
    The cosmos like a map.

Jack saw a sphere of dullest lead
    Where Saturn held his court;
He swallowed infants, it is said—
    A most phlegmatic sort.

XXXI. THE SILVER GATE

The sphere of Jupiter appeared,
    Great Emperor of all,
By gods and men obeyed and feared
    Since bringing Saturn's fall.

The sphere of Sol arose at dawn,
    A chariot of gold,
Which westward set and then was gone,
    A wonder to behold.

The sphere of Luna cast a glow,
    And silver was her light,
Illumining the land below,
    The mistress of the night.

Bright Venus winked; her sphere was green,
    This maiden on a shell;
Of ardent lovers she was queen,
    The evening star who fell.

The sphere of Mars was bloody red,
    A cause of endless pain,
Of clashing swords and wrathful dead,
    Which placed on Hell a strain.

XXXI. THE SILVER GATE

And Mercury, the final sphere
    Ruled thieves with wit and speed;
To Jack it now became quite clear
    What fate for him decreed.

The silver gate yawned opened wide,
    And Jack became the key;
Into the gate he slipped inside,
    A dark and nameless sea.

And then Jack found himself reborn,
    A golden beamish child;
Just as the sun rose in the morn,
    His fate was reconciled.

XXXII.
A Ballad for Erin

Within a graveyard late at night
    My love and I first kissed;
Her face was lit with silver light,
    The moon above our tryst.

Our hearts like roses bloomed bright red,
    Our passion fierce and strong;
Ere long we both had shared a bed,
    To her I did belong.

To her I would soon bend a knee
    To ask her for her hand;
The fairest bride of all was she,
    The fairest in the land.

In course of time we had a son,
    Half her and half of me;
Our love had now a life begun,
    And beautiful was he.

And so my love, my dearest love,
    Together we'll grow old;
Remember that the moon above
    Will warm us in the cold.

XXXII. A Ballad for Erin

Remember now that graveyard kiss,
    And where it has us led;
I could not ask for more than this
    Until we both are dead.

XXXIII.
An Elegy for Thomas Chatterton

O Rimer of Most Antient Verse,
    A cherub younge and fair,
Who duel'd the grave and got the worse
    Of that untoward affair.

O Chatterton, what hast thou done
    In poisoning that drink—
At seventeen a life undone,
    With hands still wet with ink?

Alas, now Rowley pens no more
    Of Charitie and Knights
To lift poor Thomas from his door
    In Phantasie's grand flights.

Rest well, my son; thou'st earn'd thy sleep—
    Released from all life's woes.
Thy Memorie the Poets keep;
    For thee a Slug-horn blows.

XXXIV.
The Mead of Balladry

In elden times so long ago,
    The Os warred with the Van;
Just how it ended none may know,
    Nor how the war began.

They gathered on an sacred sward
    To spit into a cask;
It is with laughter that this bard
    Now writes about their task.

Then afterwards they held a feast;
    Once foes they now were friends;
They drank each forty cups at least,
    Which helped to make amends.

All bleary-eyed when morning dawned,
    They marvelled at the spit,
For in the cask a man had spawned,
    And unsurpassed his wit.

They named him Vos, for he was both
    Of Os and of the Van,
And like a beanstalk's sudden growth,
    At night had grown a man.

XXXIV. The Mead of Balladry

Well, Vos was wise and knew all things—
    The scope of time and space;
He saw the bliss which kindness brings,
    Ineffable the grace.

The Os asked Vos to tell them things,
    Their futures so to learn,
But found such knowledge madness brings
    And caused their minds to burn.

Then Vos set out upon a quest
    For all nine worlds to see;
And in a hooded cloak he dressed
    To climb the Dreaming Tree.

He wandered to the Gates of Hell
    Upon the Ancient Track,
And entered where the dwarfs a-dwell
    In caverns foul and black.

Two brothers asked him to their home,
    To slay him in their lair;
Vos knew before he'd left to roam
    His weird would guide him there.

XXXIV. The Mead of Balladry

The dwarfs drained all poor Vos's blood
    Into a cask of mead,
So inspiration's gift would flood
    Who drank of it indeed.

Sweet ballads would like roses bud
    And blossom from the quill
Of one who drank a drop of blood
    That Vos that night would spill.

The dwarfs then quaff'd it ev'ry night
    And wrote the songs of stars;
They sang these verses with delight
    On harps and with guitars.

One day a giant came to call,
    And with him came his wife;
He little knew how soon would fall
    The ending of his life.

Their guest the dwarfs took on a boat,
    Then turned its bottom up
To settle whether giants float,
    And on him fish would sup.

XXXIV. THE MEAD OF BALLADRY

The giant's wife would weep and wail
    When she learned of his end;
The brothers' patience soon would fail,
    Their violence to portend.

One dropped a stone upon her head
    When she stepped out the door;
It cracked her skull and she fell dead,
    And then she wept no more.

Then on the dwarfs another called,
    And Sutton was his name,
The giant's son, who was appalled
    These dwarfs had brought such shame.

He rowed the dwarfs then out to sea,
    And set them on a reef,
So when the tide rose drowned would be
    These two who'd brought such grief.

The dwarfs fast struck a deal to live
    And not be drowned that day;
To Sutton they the mead would give,
    Their murders to repay.

XXXIV. The Mead of Balladry

And so the mead was Sutton's now,
    His daughter sworn to guard;
To taste a drop she'd not allow
    To dwarf or elf or bard.

But Woden wove a clever scheme
    To bring the ballads back,
And vaulted to the lands of dream,
    As quick as nimble Jack.

To Sutton's brother's home he came,
    Where slaves toiled in a field;
He told them Balework was his name,
    His true form kept concealed.

He showed the slaves a witch's stone,
    Which honed the sharpest scythe;
Into the air this stone was thrown
    With cruelty that was blithe.

They killed each other to a man:
    All nine soon fell down dead;
And that was part of Woden's plan;
    He watched them as they bled.

XXXIV. The Mead of Balladry

Then Balework all the harvest made:
    The work of nine by one;
And in return he'd asked in trade
    A drink of mead when done.

But when his brother sought this gift,
    The miser him refused,
Which opened 'twixt the two a rift,
    Their kinship badly bruised.

Then Balework gave to him a drill
    To through the mountain bore;
He turned the hellborn bit until
    He reached Old Sutton's store.

Next, Woden turned into a snake
    And slipped into the hole;
That any such a scheme could make
    This poet must extol.

Here Sutton's daughter dwelt within,
    Her lot to keep the mead;
When Woden called, so sly his grin,
    He filled her up with seed.

XXXIV. The Mead of Balladry

Three nights they dallied with delight;
    Three draughts of mead he had;
Then as an eagle he took flight
    With all the mead, the cad.

So Sutton chased him through the sky,
    He too in eagle's shape;
From world to world the two would fly—
    A treacherous escape.

In Oshome was a cask prepared
    In which the mead was spit;
With balladeers this treasure shared,
    The rest was eagle's shit.

And this is what bad poets drink,
    Who write the worst of words,
A waste of paper and of ink,
    The fashioning of turds.

XXXV.
The Jack Ring

There is a ring of gold and old
      Whose powers dæmons fear;
A talisman which I am told
      Can make one's love appear.

A Balladress had won this ring
      By playing for an elf
Who ruled the wood, an ancient king,
      And kept it for herself.

For she would call her true love, Jack,
      For whom she wandered, drear,
And played his songs upon the track
      In hopes he would appear.

I saw her once, this Balladress,
      Who strummed a black guitar.
Blood scarlet was her cloak and dress;
      Her fame had spread afar.

She played a tune which drew my tears,
      And on her hand a ring
Which she had worn for many years,
      Compelling her to sing.

XXXV. The Jack Ring

'Come back to me, my Jack, my love,
    I've searched for you so long,
And begged the moon and stars above;
    I sing you now this song.

'Your fame is wide, 'tis true, my dear,
    And many games you've won;
And many dames have shed a tear,
    When all is said and done.

'But now I bid you come to me,
    For I do wear a ring
Of stolen elfin gold, you see,
    And it your love will bring.'

I saw upon the Ring old runes,
    A script forgotten, gone,
As eldritch as the singer's tunes;
    A dream-door gave a yawn.

From out of it stepped Jack himself,
    A spritely grinning imp;
He danced a clog just like an elf,
    Though I discerned a limp.

XXXV. The Jack Ring

A thousand years or more he was,
    Though almost just a boy;
I smiled to see him then because
    His mischief brought me joy.

Then when the song was done he said:
    'Why have you called me here?'
Jack doffed the hat from off his head
    And cocked a pointy ear.

'Why, I would be your darling wife,'
    The Balladress replied.
'Together we would share a life
    Until we both have died.'

'A silly goose you are, my sweet.'
    He took her by the hand.
'Upstairs let's go and merry meet,
    And I'll show you Jack's Land.'

And then they left me all alone:
    For company, an ale.
While high above a full moon shone
    With spectral light, and pale.

XXXVI.
On Hallowe'en

On Hallowe'en the witches ride,
  The bogies wander free,
And that is when you must decide
  On which side you will be.

On Hallowe'en a faery light
  Appears within the bog;
You'll see it dancing in the night,
  In swirling veils of fog.

Come children guising down the street,
  Their bellies for to fill
With cakes and custard good to eat;
  Refuse them if you will,

But stark misfortune will you court
  From lubberkin and imp,
Who with such misers make their sport
  With those who hoard and scrimp.

Believe you me, for I was one,
  And would not tithe my due;
Your misery will not be done
  Until the cock has crew.

XXXVI. On Hallowe'en

On Hallowe'en your only chance
    To make it through the night
Is letting witches have their dance
    By Jack-a-Lanthorn's light.

XXXVII.
The Scarlet Balladress

There was a Scarlet Balladress
    Who walked the Ancient Track;
She wore a scarlet cloak and dress,
    And only sang of Jack.

She played upon a black guitar
    With haunted silver strings,
Whose sounds were eldritch, most bizarre,
    As were the songs she sings.

This instrument was very old,
    A Devil's gift I've heard;
Or that is how the story's told,
    The consequence inferred.

She always sang a tale of Jack
    Upon her black guitar,
And sought him on the Ancient Track,
    To her a northern star,

Until the night she tracked him down
    And took him to her bed;
She quickly doffed her scarlet gown:
    For him her legs were spread.

XXXVII. THE SCARLET BALLADRESS

Jack disappeared into her quim,
    As though he were unborn,
And nevermore she saw of him
    When dawned the fateful morn.

No longer did she search for Jack,
    For now she was her love,
And wandered on the Ancient Track,
    A spectral moon above.

XXXVIII.
Beneath the Eildon Tree

I lolled beneath the Eildon Tree
  One drowsy summer's day
In hopes I would a Rhymer be
  With prophecies to say.

The Queen of Elfland soon arrove
  To find me lazing there,
And gestured me into her grove,
  This lady bright and fair.

Entranced, I had to follow her,
  To ride her milk-white steed;
Such passions did my lady stir,
  I felt a burning need,

An urge that made me a subject to
  Her realm ethereal,
And led me henceforth to eschew
  All things material.

I stayed in Elfland moments—years—
  A land of utter bliss;
A place where ballads brought me tears
  And lovers long would kiss.

XXXVIII. BENEATH THE EILDON TREE

In time from there I had to leave,
    As mortals all must do;
But enigmatic Fate would weave
    A thread of Faerie through

My life, which never was the same
    As those who merely toiled
And ate and slept: a pointless game.
    From labour I recoiled,

Save writing verses for my Queen,
    Which flowed fast from my quill;
I ache to find that Eildon Green—
    I wander searching still.

XXXIX.
The Weird of the Two Sisters

Jack set out for the witch's wood
    Where Eleanora dwelt—
A place folk shunned as well they should,
    For bone-bred fear they felt.

But Jack was not just any man,
    And held the Eildon Sword;
He prayed before his quest began
    That he might keep his word.

The sword shone with a daemon light,
    A lanthorn in the dark,
Which guided Jack into the night,
    A faithful devil's spark.

Jack came upon a crackling fire
    Where warmed a balladeer
Who strummed a silver stringèd lyre,
    Quite haunting to the ear.

This harp was made from human bones
    Fished from a river's bed,
And issued sighs and longing moans
    In spite of being dead.

XXXIX. The Weird of the Two Sisters

The balladeer, greybearded, old,
    With crooked fingers played
The strings while maudlin stories told,
    A most peculiar trade.

He sang of sisters who one day
    Strolled by the river bank;
One pushed the other in they say,
    And like a stone she sank.

Well, Eleanora did this deed
    To steal poor Elspeth's groom,
And planted then the blackest seed
    To sprout and bring her doom.

For at the wedding came a bard
    Who played a haunted harp:
A moment that was cruelly starred,
    An irony most sharp.

There Elspeth's bones to all explained
    How she had met her death,
And Eleanora's soul was stained;
    The guests all held their breath.

XXXIX. The Weird of the Two Sisters

She fled the hall in tears of shame,
    To dwell in witch's wood—
A sorceress of growing fame,
    Who found in evil good.

She stole a sapphire from a duke,
    The Ballad Stone of lore,
Which earned the Faerie Queen's rebuke:
    It only spurred her more.

She asked if Jack would be her groom
    To reign as queen and king,
A reign to spell the final doom,
    For chaos they would bring.

But Jack was nimble, Jack was quick,
    And swung the Eildon sword;
For up his sleeve he had a trick
    To let him keep his word.

He struck the sapphire with his blade
    Of goblin steel and keen;
By Wayland Smith it had been made,
    The finest ever seen.

XXXIX. THE WEIRD OF THE TWO SISTERS

The Ballad Stone to pieces flew,
　　With such a mighty crash;
The haunted harp then split in two,
　　The witch was burnt to ash.

And so the bones set Elspeth free
　　To fly up to the sky,
But not our Jack, a rambler, he,
　　Whose wit was ever spry.

XL.
The Ettin under Beacon Hill

On Acorn Street, on Beacon Hill,
    There was a door so black,
Who passed it by would feel a chill
    And never once look back.

Jack gave the door a little knock,
    A second and a third,
Whilst far away a church's clock
    Chimed twelve times that he heard.

The door creaked open just a crack
    Ere yawning all the way;
A gaunt man fixed his eyes on Jack,
    A predator his prey.

Inviting Jack to come inside,
    This man was pale and cold,
Like one who long ago had died
    But earth would not enfold.

A book lay spread upon a desk
    And on the page a rune,
Suggesting rites and arts grotesque
    Performed beneath the moon.

XL. The Ettin under Beacon Hill

Jack had been summoned by this man,
  If man indeed he was,
This warlock with a wicked plan
  To slacken Satan's jaws.

A passage gaped, a hellish mouth,
  Which tempted Jack within;
It thirsted for his soul, a drouth
  Engendered by his sin.

A winding stair led down and down
  Into the dark and cold—
A cavern under Boston Town,
  A heathen place of old.

There, chained upon a toppled stone,
  The exiled god of lies,
Who said to Jack: 'My, how you've grown;
  'I see you have my eyes.'

Jack noticed then the captive's shoes,
  Which were of goblins' craft;
His sidelong looks did so amuse
  Bound Lokkey that he laughed.

XL. The Ettin under Beacon Hill

'Sure, take my shoes, my son, my Jack,
　　To help you in your quest;
Yea, wear them well upon your track;
　　I think it for the best.

'And just one thing, when you are done:
　　Return and loose my chains;
Come, be a faithful loving son—
　　Reward me for my pains.'

The goblin shoes that Jack put on
　　Each pointed at the toe;
He left the cave an ettin's spawn,
　　Which he was loath to know.

XLI.
Jack's Silver Key

Long centuries old Jack had trod
    The dry and dusty road,
And wandered o'er the length of Nod
    Where ancient gods abode,

Until he found a willow tree
    Whose back stooped where it stood;
Beneath its fronds Jack knew would be
    A path into the wood.

He played tantivy on his horn
    And traipsed into the wild,
While years from him like wool were shorn,
    Until he felt a child.

He came upon a vacant church,
    All overgrown with thorn,
The object of Jack's weary search—
    The place where he'd been born.

He went into the hallowed ground
    Where slept the faithful dead,
And took a shovel that he found
    Propped up against a shed.

XLI. Jack's Silver Key

Jack dug into the cold dark earth,
    Marked by a rain-smoothed stone,
A task that brought him little mirth,
    And vowed he would atone.

Beneath the earth a coffin was,
    Hexagonal in shape,
And spurred on by his fiendish cause,
    Jack pulled the lid agape.

Inside, the corpse of his old friend
    In putrefaction lay,
And little else could more offend
    Than what he smelled that day.

A box was clutched in long-dead hands—
    Jack loosed their ghoulish hold;
He'd hunted it through many lands,
    A thousand years I'm told.

Inside the box a silver key,
    The silver key to dream;
Jack knew that it would set him free—
    His soul it would redeem.

XLI. Jack's Silver Key

With reverence he scooped the soil
    To lay upon his friend;
Jack took some comfort that his toil
    Would soon be at an end.

A raven perched upon a tree
    And fixed his eyes on Jack;
Its name I've heard is Memory,
    A spectre winged and black.

Jack left his lanthorn by the church
    To go upon his way;
There you may find it if you search—
    It flickers still, some say.

XLII.
Death and the Balladress

The Balladress roamed far and wide
    And sang in lonesome inns,
Where drunkards heard her songs and sighed,
    Reminded of their sins.

One night she strummed her black guitar
    And saw a doomful sight:
Grim Death himself stood at the bar,
    Half dark and half in light.

The Balladress then played a song
    She'd learned once from a witch,
And Death began to sing along,
    His bony legs to twitch.

'I met an old man by the way,
    His beard was long and white;
His coat a myrtle shade of grey—
    I feared to catch a sight.

'My name is Death, 'tis plain to see:
    Who turns all flesh to dust;
Lords, dukes, and ladies bow to me,
    And likewise so thou must.'

XLII. DEATH AND THE BALLADRESS

'I'll give you silver and my gold;
　　I'll give you all my store,
For I am not so very old
　　And wish to live some more.'

'Fair maid, your beauty cast aside,
　　For now your time has come;
No longer glory in your pride,
　　Not worth the smallest crumb.'

And at her tomb a lover cried:
　　'Here lies a fair young maid
Who long before her time hath died,
　　For Death her wish betrayed.'

Such glee Death took to hear this tune,
　　He spared the singer's life;
To ever wander was her boon,
　　To Death, some said, a wife.

XLIII.
Jack in Xanadu

Jack wandered far, far to the east,
　　Where few had gone, not man or beast,
To win some gold, a tale at least,
　　Which he might tell at some king's feast.

And there he found it: Xanadu,
　　A ruin now it lay,
Whose former shape he could construe
　　Neath æons of decay.

It was a place where dreamers met
　　To hear a phantom lyre,
To drink a drug and to forget
　　The ache of their desire.

Jack thought he glimpsed a scarlet ghost
　　Who strummed a black guitar,
The damsel who had loved him most;
　　He heard her from afar.

'I sang for thee, O golden hair,
　　My lovely blue-eyed Jack;
There never lived a man as fair,
　　But I am dead, alack!'

XLIII. JACK'S IN XANADU

Upon the ground Jack found a vial,
    Unstoppered it to drink,
To let the opium beguile
    And into dreams to sink.

Dream is a land close by to death
    Where Jack his lover found;
Tantivy was his shibboleth
    And made his horn resound.

They shared a single night, these two,
    A night of scarlet sin,
Until they had to bid adieu
    To that romantic inn.

In Xanadu Jack then awoke
    Upon a bed of stone,
And shivering, dew-drenched his cloak,
    Once more he was alone.

XLIV.
The Ballad of Molly Craftwell

(elsewise known as Molly Whuppie)

I sing the tale of Molly's craft,
    The youngest girl of three;
Her sisters thought that she was daft
    And taunted her with glee.

Their mother turned them out of home
    With only crusts of bread,
Upon the Ancient Track to roam
    In hopes that they would wed.

Her sisters tied poor Molly to
    A knotted Scotch elm tree;
When down a crow from heaven flew
    Who pecked to set her free;

For she was blessed upon her brow,
    And at her back the wind;
She caught up with her sisters now,
    Their ill will to rescind.

They reached at length a ruined keep
    Where dwelt a giant's brood,

XLIV. The Ballad of Molly Craftwell

And asked there for a place to sleep,
    Perhaps a bite of food.

They claimed a servant Molly was
    Who'd wash and scrub the pot;
She bore this injury because
    She reckoned it her lot.

The giant's wife fed them some meat
    And put them all to bed,
When came the giant's stomping feet,
    And this is what he said:

'O fee and fie! O fo and fum!
    Warm British blood I smell;
I wish it were inside my tum,
    My hunger for to quell . . .'

The giant's daughters with them slept,
    His pale and treasured pearls,
And in the dark he softly crept
    To snatch the newcome girls.

Around the giant's daughters' necks
    Hung glinting golden chains,
But Molly switched them to perplex
    The giant's feeble brains.

The lackwit ate his daughters' flesh
    And drank their blood like wine;
So sweet they tasted, warm and fresh,
    Like winter's slaughtered swine.

The sisters fled this ghastly lair
    And ran in fear all night;
They crossed a bridge of one gold hair,
    Which aided in their flight.

At last they came to Ettinfell,
    The fabled House of Drake,
Once built by Jack with bricks from Hell,
    That spry and crafty rake.

Of Molly's tale the Squire was fond
    And offered her a deal:
His eldest son in wedded bond
    If she a purse could steal.

XLIV. The Ballad of Molly Craftwell

And so that night did Molly dare
    To poach the giant's purse;
She crossed the bridge of one gold hair,
    A heroic is the verse.

A second son the Squire pledged
    If she could rob a ring,
And Molly's triumph is alleged
    By this the rime I sing.

Her elder sisters each a Drake,
    A station which they crew,
The Squire promised he would make
    A Drake of Molly too,

If she could steal the Sword of Light
    Behind the giant's bed,
And then across the bridge take flight,
    Lest she be ground for bread.

Now this time when she took the sword
    The giant gave her chase;
His titan legs could haste afford,
    While she could scarce keep pace.

XLIV. The Ballad of Molly Craftwell

Then to the golden hair she came
    And crossed it with great speed;
The giant could not do the same,
    Which forced him to concede.

But Molly would not be a wife,
    And kept instead the sword;
She chose to lead a rambler's life,
    Which freedom could afford.

So now my tale of Molly's done;
    I trust it pleased you some;
Much fame and fortune has she won;
    Her tales have scarce begun.

XLV.
Molly Craftwell
&
The Devil

*
*
* * *
*

A Folk-Horror for Marionettes

*** Dramatis Personae ***

MOLLY CRAFTWELL, a treader on the track
EZEKIEL WHITLOCK, a balladeer and Heaven's clerk
JACK, a tale-told rake
BETTY CROW, a formless apparition
THEOBALD CRAFTWELL, a writer of grotesque phantasies
SCRATCH, the Devil himself

* * * *

The Place: The Land of Nod
The Time: The Days of Yore

ACT ONE

Scene: The Toad and Crow, an inn by the crossing of ways.
Enter WHITLOCK the Balladeer.

WHITLOCK: By Homer's beard in dark we meet:
My followers, though few,
Hark to my words for they are sweet,
And neither lies nor true.

I sing to you of Molly's craft,
The youngest girl of three;
Her sisters thought that she was daft,
And taunted her with glee.

Until she won a giant's hoard,
A feat none else would dare;
Her tricks earned her a witch's sword,
And golden was her hair.

But Molly would not wed the prince,
And set off down the track
To have adventures ever since,
Just like that scoundrel Jack.

Until she came unto an inn,
Where road criss-crossed with way;
It was a place of scarlet sin,
Or so the Christians say.

Exit WHITLOCK. Enter MOLLY.

MOLLY: Hell's teeth! I'm chilled right to the core;
I pray I find a bed
To rest my bones and feet so sore,
A pillow for my head.

SCRATCH: Good eventide, my pretty one;
Perchance you'd like some wine?
Your hair is golden like the sun,
So brightly does it shine!

MOLLY: Now that's a line I've heard before
From men with a design
To treat me like a common whore
And ply me with cheap wine.

SCRATCH: You wound me, miss; you cut me deep,
And cause me to feel pain.
I do not think you one so cheap
To sell herself for gain.

MOLLY: Well then, good sir, I have to ask
What do you want from me?
It does not take my wit to task
Your interest to see.

SCRATCH: I only want to please you, dear;
My motives are quite plain.
Your heart's desire to me is clear,
Pray show me not disdain—

True love perhaps? A house and home,
A place to rest your feet,
No longer having a need to roam,
Your life so incomplete?

MOLLY: 'Tis true my life upon the road
Betimes on me doth weigh;
But never could you ever goad
Me in one place to stay.

If you could give me but one wish,
I'd ask for just a bed,
A cut of beef upon a dish,
A pillow for my head.

SCRATCH: Why, nothing more would I enjoy,
Your wish for me to grant;
Perhaps in bed you'd like a boy,
So warmth will not be scant.

MOLLY: You rascal, Scratch, I would indeed . . .
A night I'll have with Jack!
And once I have fulfilled my need,
I'll set off down the track.

SCRATCH: By Azathoth, this wish I grant:
A bed and meat and Jack;
A dark spell now I shall incant
Perhaps you should stand back . . .

Alakazam! Alakazoo!
O Yog-Sothoth, I call on you!
I summon Dumah, lord of lies,
Beelzebub, the god of flies,

To Molly Craftwell I confer
The Jack-a-tales to bed with her.

Exit SCRATCH. Enter JACK.

JACK: I hear that you have summoned Jack,
And that would be my name,
A fellow treader on the track,
I see we are the same.

MOLLY: In many ways we differ, sir,
In ways below the belt;
And in that place I must aver
A warmth I've never felt.

[166]

JACK:	Perhaps this warmth we should explore
	Upstairs in solitude,
	Where we can close and bolt the door,
	And niceties occlude.

MOLLY:	I'd hoped to have a bite to eat;
	No matter, let's a-bed!
	Instead we'll feast on other meat,
	And moan to raise the dead . . .
	Exit MOLLY AND JACK.
	Close curtain.

ACT TWO

Scene: A darken'd wood. There is a single gravestone here, inscribed with the name BETTY CROW.

Enter MOLLY.

MOLLY:	Oh, grandmother, I am a fool
	To trade away my soul
	To such a tattered greedy ghoul
	For such a fleeting goal.
	Enter SCRATCH.

SCRATCH:	A ghoul am I? Now that is rude;
	My word did I not keep?
	'Twas you whose wishes were so crude;
	Too late it is to weep.

MOLLY:	Begone, you hound of Hell, you imp;
	No more on this I'll dwell.
	No more I'll watch you preen and primp;
	Returneth now to Hell!

SCRATCH: I'll go for now, but come what may,
            To Hell with me you'll go.
            Your soul belongs to me I say;
            A debt to me you owe.

Exit Scratch.
Enter BETTY CROW, a floating disembodied ghost.

BETTY: Do not despair, my Molly dear,
            Your soul is not yet lost.
            Of Scratch you need to have no fear;
            You do so at a cost.

MOLLY: My grandmother, O is that you,
            Who calls across the veil?
            Is this a vision that is true,
            Or do my senses fail?

BETTY: 'Tis Betty Crow who speaketh now,
            From out of blackest death,
            Although I cannot tell you how,
            For I do not draw breath.

MOLLY: What shall I do? Show me a way
            That does not lead to Hell.
            I do not wish my soul to pay
            And in the flames to dwell.

BETTY: There is another way to tread,
            My bright and gold-haired child,
            Between the living and dead,
            Like flowers that are wild.

MOLLY: But what of Scratch and of his claim—
            How shall I deal with him?

I struck a bargain to my shame
Upon a flagrant whim.

BETTY: I know Old Scratch from long ago;
He is the Black Elf King.
One's secret wishes he will know,
And so temptation bring,

Much like the thorn he can ensnare
You in his bony touch;
So you must be a cunning hare
Escaping from his clutch.

And when your flight comes to an end
To reach the mouth of Hell,
Take you this sword: a witch's friend,
For devils can it fell.

Cue: Lower sword.
Close curtain.

ACT THREE

Scene: The Gates of Heaven. An angel stands before a lectern, upon which sits a hallowed book. The angel bears a striking resemblance to WHITLOCK the Bard.

Enter Theobald CRAFTWELL.

CRAFTWELL: My sainted aunt, what madness this?
I was just now a-bed,
And dreaming of a mother's kiss—
Perchance I now am dead?

WHITLOCK: Alas, I fear, 'tis as you say;
Thy span hath reached its end,

For mortals all must have their day,
Stagnation to forfend.

CRAFTWELL: My ballads though, will they endure
Until the end of things?
Of this one fact can you assure?—
To me it comfort brings.

WHITLOCK: Your words indeed will linger on,
But then they too shall fade,
As words that on the sand are drawn,
And castles children made.

CRAFTWELL: This truth, alas, I cannot bear;
I must have made a mark!
Like emeralds my words are rare;
They glitter in the dark.

WHITLOCK: All things must have an end, good sir,
As autumn leaves must fall;
Why, of this truth you must concur,
That change is good for all.

CRAFTWELL: Nay, to that law I shall not bend,
And crave forever more
My verses shall not find an end,
Surviving in folk's lore.

Enter SCRATCH.

SCRATCH: Pray let me introduce myself:
Old Solomon, my name;
Some call me goblin, some an elf—
A devil, just the same.

WHITLOCK: Begone from here, you loathsome beast;
              From Heaven's Gate, away!
              I'll not allow a demon priest
              Upon this soul to prey.

SCRATCH: You know the rules as well do I;
              The game is still in play.
              I still can claim those by the by
              Who have just died to-day.

              So hear me out, as Faust once did:
              I offer you a deal;
              For your immortal soul I bid,
              A passionate appeal.

              To see your verses outlast doom,
              Just take my bony hand;
              No time or tide shall then consume
              Your marks upon the sand.

CRAFTWELL: This fruit you offer me is sweet;
              How can I not bite in?—
              Although the will of God I cheat,
              Which is the gravest sin.

              I do! I do! I'll take your hand,
              And follow you to Hell,
              That dark and gloomy distant land,
              Eternally to dwell.

Exit CRAFTWELL and SCRATCH.
[WHITLOCK: Oh, bugger!]
Close curtain.

ACT FOUR

Scene: Ye Hell-mouth. Brimstone and perdition lie beyond this toothy maw.
Enter Craftwell.

CRAFTWELL: Was I too quick my fate to seal,
And make my mark in wax?
With Satan have I struck a deal,
And pay a heavy tax . . .

Enter SCRATCH.

SCRATCH: In truth you were an easy mark,
And lacking much in sport;
My scheme to lead you to the dark
You did not try to thwart.

Exit Scratch.
Enter MOLLY.

MOLLY: Hell's teeth indeed, for here I am—
The mouth of Hell yawns wide.
Led to the slaughter like a lamb,
What horrors wait inside?

CRAFTWELL: Is that my golden-headed niece
Before me that I see,
Whose infant squalls gave little peace
When dandled on my knee?

MOLLY: O Uncle, tell me, is it thou?
Two kindred, we are lost!
A curse upon our blood, I vow;
Why must we pay this cost?

CRAFTWELL: An ancestor I fear it was,
             Who practiced heathen craft,
             And doomed his offspring to the jaws
             Of Satan while he laughed.

MOLLY: We are not fettered by our fate;
             Another way I know.
             She taught me to how to slip Hell's gate,
             My grannie, Betty Crow.
             Enter SCRATCH.

SCRATCH: I fear escape is not to be;
             Two Craftwells now I doom.
             Into hell's jaws now come with me,173173173f
             For darkness must consume!

MOLLY: I conjure up my witch's sword,
             Inscribed with elder runes,
             Which to the Devil are a ward,
             However much he croons.

Lower sword, the blade pointing towards SCRATCH to repel him offstage.
Exit SCRATCH.

             Raise sword.

SCRATCH: (from offstage)
             So be it then! Your soul I shall not claim;
             Your uncle's soul although . . .

A shepherd's crook enters the stage from the side and hooks CRAFT-
WELL's body.

CRAFTWELL: Alas, I bear my forebear's shame,
             Which drags me down below.
             The crook pulls CRAFTWELL offstage.

But do not weep for me, my dear;
My verses shall live on,
Declaimed by bard and balladeer,
Until the final dawn.

Exit Craftwell.
Enter WHITLOCK.

WHITLOCK: Like steel your mettle meets its test,
Forgiven now your sin;
You routed Satan with such zest—
A bold resounding win!

In Heaven's kingdom take your place,
O Molly, bright and gold,
Of keenest wit and fair of face,
Your tale forever told.

MOLLY: I thank thee, sir, but I decline,
And choose another way;
Not God's or Hell's, my path is mine,
Just like the Queen of Fae.

Exit MOLLY.
[SCRATCH: (offstage) Better luck next time, Ezekiel.]
Close curtain.

XLVI.
To Sing for Jack

The Balladress to highlands went
    To sing her witching tune,
Which into æther echoes sent,
    An auditory rune.

As ever did she sing for Jack,
    Her one and only love,
Who wandered on the Ancient Track
    'Neath moon and stars above.

But rather than that pretty elf,
    There came to call on her
A bony spectre, Death himself,
    Who gave a cattish purr.

'Take me to be your husband now,
    Your faithful loving groom;
My love for thee must be enow,
    For here you meet your doom.'

Her black guitar lay in a field,
    An eldritch devil's thing;
Who plays it finds her fate is sealed
    Forever then to sing

XLVI. TO SING FOR JACK

For Jack, for Jack, to sing for Jack,
A passion burning true,
And yet it is a fate most black;
Perhaps it will be you.

Acknowledgments

"The Ballad Stone," in *32 White Horses on a Vermillion Hill* (Planet X Publications, 2019).

"Ballads for the Witching Hour," *The Audient Void No. 7* (2019)

"The Black Hunt," *Spectral Realms* No. 8 (Winter 2018).

"Cat's Paw," *The Audient Void* No. 3 (2017).

"Cruel Eleanora," *Spectral Realms* No. 11 (Summer 2019).

"The Duke of Balladry," *Spectral Realms* No. 11 (Summer 2019).

"The Haunting Bones," *Spectral Realms* No. 10 (Winter 2019).

Yᵉ Historie of Jack of Lanthorne (chapbook) (Jackanapes Press, 2017).

"Jack and the Devil," *The Audient Void* No 4 (2017).

"Jack in Xanadu," *Spectral Realms* No. 12 (Winter 2020).

"The Jack of Cats," *The Audient Void* No. 2 (2016).

"The King of Cats," *The Audient Void* No. 1 (2016).

"Mad Jack-a-Lee," *Spectral Realms* No. 10 (Winter 2019).

"A Page from Jack's Diary," in *Diary of a Sorceress* by Ashley Dioses (Hippocampus Press, 2017).

"The Queen of Cats," *The Audient Void* No. 6 (2018).

"The Scarlet Balladress," *The Audient Void* No. 5 (2018) (as "Jack Yᵉ Balladeer").